Every technology professional needs to prepare for the quantum era. This accessible guide is a must-read, providing the essential foundation to understand the shift and ask the right strategic questions.

Rashik Parmar MBE, *Former Group CEO, BCS, The Chartered Institute for IT*

A clear and modern introduction that effectively conveys quantum computing fundamentals, ideal for computer scientists and related disciplines. Excellent algorithms and cryptography overviews, thoughtful technology framing and a forward-looking perspective that sparks curiosity.

Aniello Esposito, *Principal Research Engineer, Hewlett Packard Enterprise*

An accessible, sharp and brilliantly insightful guide to quantum computing that cuts through the hype to reveal what it really means in practice. A must-read for anyone serious about the next computing frontier.

Boby Jose, *Author of 'Test Automation', and Test Strategy and Transformation Leader*

An accessible and practical introduction to quantum computing. It covers the fundamentals and the new opportunities to solve problems with this technology, providing a solid foundation to apply it in real projects and deliver value to stakeholders. Highly recommended for business analysts.

Gottfried Szing, *Senior Business Analyst*

GETTING STARTED WITH QUANTUM COMPUTING

An introduction to tech and coding transformation, and societal impact

Edited by James Davenport

CONTENTS

ABOUT THE AUTHORS

Oli Cox works in fintech and has experience applying quantum computing and emerging technologies to real-world problems in financial services. He holds an MSci in Theoretical Physics from Imperial College London, where he specialised in quantum mechanics.

James Davenport is Hebron and Medlock Professor of Information Technology at the University of Bath, where he leads the teaching of quantum computing. He is treasurer of the BCS Quantum Computing specialist group and sits on quantum standardisation bodies at national, European and international level. He is FBCS and Honorary FBCS.

David Galvin (*Daithí Ó Gealbháin*) is a Quantum Software Engineer on the Advanced Computing and Emerging Technologies team at Hartree Centre, part of STFC. He completed his MSc in Quantum Science and Technology at Trinity College Dublin, Ireland and has a background in Mathematical Sciences. As part of his work, he investigates the emerging use cases for quantum technologies to assess its viability for problems in UK science and industry.

Marco Ugo Gambetta MsC in Mathematics, started in KPMG as a quantum expert and built most of the services that are provided today. He worked in many projects across the quantum technology landscape, some of the more remarkable are the delivery of the first QKD link outside the lab in the Nordics and the collaboration in the EU consortium POLIIICE for the study of how quantum technology can support law enforcement in the fight against organised crime and terrorism.

Michael Garn obtained his PhD from Brunel University. This work was undertaken while he was a Quantum Software Engineer at the Hartree Centre, UK.

Jeremy Green is a Security Architect with Leidos and RAF Cyber Reservist with over 20 industry certifications, including CISSP, CISM, CEH, CASP+ and CHFI. A certified instructor and researcher, he is completing a PhD in Computer Science where he is developing the Q_SLICE quantum threat model and the QUNATA quantum cybersecurity framework and readiness score.

Jessica Jones, PhD, is a Principal Research Engineer in the HPE/AI EMEA Research Lab of Hewlett Packard Enterprise and is based in Bristol. Her current research topics of interest include telecommunications, digital twins, quantum computing, performance engineering and cryptography. Novel architectures and accelerators feature prominently in her work.

Jamie Kavanagh is a public sector strategist leading inclusion and community cohesion for Oxfordshire. He specialises in the intersection of emergent technology and ethics, and sit on the committee for BCS specialist group for quantum computing.

Stefano Mensa was, at the time of writing, the strategic lead for quantum computing and emerging technologies at the STFC Hartree Centre, a UK-based national laboratory and supercomputing centre focused on applying advanced computing to solve major industry challenges. In this role, he defined and delivered the Centre's roadmap to help translate research into real-world, scalable impact. Across his career, Stefano has been committed to enabling the quantum computing community, particularly around applications and quantum-classical integration. Stefano holds a PhD in Theoretical Chemistry from the University of Liverpool, where he is also an Honorary Senior Research Fellow.

Josie Woolham is a Quantum Senior Consultant at KPMG Australia, focusing on quantum computing applications and quantum cyber risk. She holds an MSci in Mathematics from the University of Bristol, where she developed a strong foundation in quantum information theory and quantum computation.

FOREWORD

Quantum computing is currently at the early adopter stage that arguably generative AI, that other enigmatic technology, was at some five years ago – just before we started reading about it and making our first fumbled prompts for ChatGPT. The answers obtained were, as often as not, even more fumbled!

In the intervening period large language models (LLMs) have improved exponentially to the point that we can now have a meaningful dialogue on just about any appropriate topic and feel that we are actually speaking to a friendly, albeit well-informed, peer. Of course, such anthropomorphism is largely a mirage, the LLM providing a statistically driven harvest of information that already exists out there, then tying it in a pretty bow to make it sound 'convincingly' human.

Right now, there is no beautifully intuitive interface for 'newbies' to engage with quantum computing in a similarly (pseudo-)conversational manner. With this in mind, there is no shortcut to the spadework of learning some basic terminology and concepts from quantum physics to get to the point of understanding how a quantum bit, or qubit, differs from a 'conventional' binary digit, or for understanding how quantum computing, to borrow a phrase from the brewing industry, reaches the parts others cannot reach. It is for this reason that I commend this book, alongside other resources such as from the Open University's free short course on quantum computing or BCS Quantum Computing specialist group events, to anybody from a STEM background who wishes to inform themselves about this nascent technology.

Julian Fletcher FBCS
Chairman, BCS Quantum Computing specialist group

1 INTRODUCTION TO QUANTUM COMPUTING

James Davenport and Jeremy Green

WHAT IS QUANTUM COMPUTING?

Quantum computing represents a fundamental shift in how we process information. Rather than using the classical binary digits (bits) found in traditional computers, quantum computers harness the strange and counterintuitive behaviour of quantum mechanics to perform calculations in entirely new ways.

QUANTUM MECHANICS

To understand quantum computing, we first need to appreciate the quantum world itself. Quantum mechanics is a fundamental theory in physics that describes the behaviour of nature at and below the scale of atoms. The theory was developed in the early 1900s, when experiments began revealing results that defied classical explanation.

In our everyday experience, what physicists call **classical mechanics**, objects exist in a specific place at a specific time. A tennis ball thrown at a wall will bounce back predictably, every single time. But in the quantum realm, this certainty dissolves into probability. That same tennis ball, if it were a quantum object, would have a probability of bouncing back from the wall, but also a chance of appearing on the other side of the wall, or even emerging from the other side. Particles exist not in single locations but as clouds of possibility until the moment they are measured.

This probabilistic nature isn't a limitation of our knowledge – it's a fundamental feature of how the universe works at its smallest scales.

BITS TO QUBITS

A classical computer stores information in **bits**, each of which can be either a 0 or a 1. Physically, these bits are switches (transistors) that are either on or off. All of classical computing, from smartphone apps to supercomputer simulations, is built from this simple foundation.

A quantum computer, by contrast, uses **qubits** (quantum bits). Like a classical bit, a qubit can represent 0 or 1. But crucially, it can also exist in a **superposition** of both states simultaneously. Think of a coin spinning in the air: while it's spinning, it's not quite heads and not quite tails, but a combination of both possibilities. Only when it lands (when we **measure** it) does it become definitively one or the other.

This superposition property is the source of quantum computing's potential power. A register of classical bits can represent only one specific number out of the total possibilities at any given moment. A register of qubits, however, can exist in a superposition of all those possibilities simultaneously. This means the computational state space grows exponentially with each added qubit.

For example, while 30 classical bits can represent any single value from a set of about a billion (2^{30}), 30 qubits in a carefully prepared superposition can represent all of those billion values at once. This inherent parallelism is what allows a quantum algorithm to explore a vast number of potential solutions in a single computational step.

However, a crucial constraint prevents us from simply reading out this vast parallel state. Schrödinger's cat analogy, where the cat is considered both dead and alive until its box is opened, perfectly illustrates the quantum principles of superposition and measurement, as discussed in Chapter 3 regarding how a qubit can exist in a combination of states until it is observed. The laws of quantum mechanics dictate that when we observe a qubit (the act of measurement), its superposition collapses. It must yield a definite classical outcome, forcing it to become either a 0 or a 1.

Therefore, the art of quantum algorithm design, as introduced in Chapters 3 and 4, lies in cleverly manipulating these superpositions. The goal is to orchestrate interference patterns among the parallel computational paths to amplify the 'probability amplitudes' of the correct answers while cancelling out the wrong ones. Only after this carefully crafted evolution is the system measured, collapsing the superposition and yielding the desired solution with high probability.

THE BLOCH SPHERE: VISUALISING A QUBIT

The state of a single qubit is often visualised using the **Bloch sphere**, a geometric representation where the north pole represents state $|0\rangle$,[1] the south pole represents state $|1\rangle$, and every point on the sphere's surface represents a possible superposition state (see Figure 1.1). Quantum operations (gates) appear as rotations of this sphere, moving the qubit's state around the surface. When we measure the qubit, its state collapses to either the north or south pole and we get either a 0 or a 1, with probabilities determined by how close to that pole the state was before measurement. This will help us visualise the gates and circuits discussed later in the book.

ENTANGLEMENT

Qubits have another remarkable property that classical bits lack: **entanglement**. When two qubits become entangled, their fates are linked in such a way that the state of one cannot be described independently of the other. Measuring one instantly affects the other, even if they are physically separated by vast

---

1 See Chapter 4 for more on this representation of qubit states.

Figure 1.1 Bloch sphere[2] (A qubit is represented as a point on the Bloch sphere, and its angle θ from the |0⟩ axis determines the probability of collapsing to |0⟩ or |1⟩ when measured)

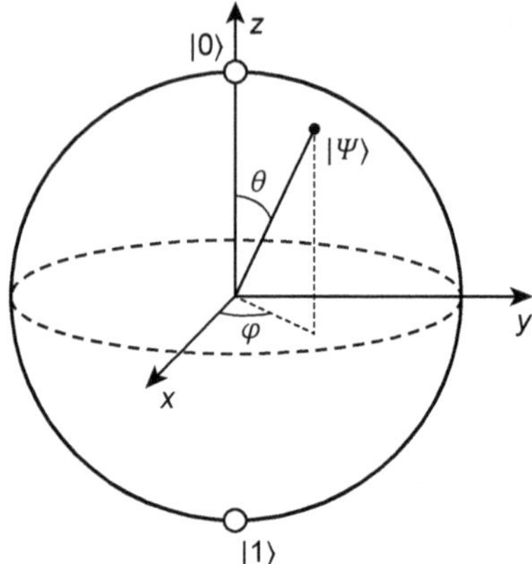

distances. Einstein famously called this 'spooky action at a distance'.

Entanglement is what allows quantum computers to create extremely complex correlations between qubits, enabling them to tackle problems that would be impossible for classical machines.

NISQ

The term that best captures the present moment in quantum computing was coined by the theoretical physicist John Preskill in his influential 2018 paper, 'Quantum computing in the NISQ era and beyond'. Preskill introduced the acronym NISQ, which stands for 'noisy intermediate-scale quantum'.

2 By Smite-Meister, CC BY-SA 3.0, commons.wikimedia.org/wiki/File:Bloch_sphere.svg.

As Preskill explained, 'intermediate scale' refers to quantum processors with between roughly fifty and a few hundred qubits. This scale is significant because it is the threshold where quantum computers may be able to perform specialised tasks that surpass the capabilities of today's classical supercomputers – a milestone often referred to as 'quantum supremacy' or 'quantum advantage'.

However, the 'noisy' part of NISQ points to the single biggest challenge facing the field. Qubits are extremely sensitive to their environment. Heat, electromagnetic radiation and even vibrations can cause decoherence (the collapse of superposition states) before a computation is complete. This means that the quantum gates we use to perform calculations are error prone.

This noise means that today's quantum computers produce errors. As Preskill noted, while NISQ devices with 50–100 qubits may be useful tools for exploring many-body quantum physics and other scientific questions, 'the 100-qubit quantum computer will not change the world right away'. These machines can perform calculations that demonstrate quantum principles, but they cannot yet run the long, complex algorithms like Shor's algorithm (see Chapter 4) for factoring large numbers (which would deliver the full promise of quantum advantage for applications like code breaking – see Chapter 6).

Preskill emphasised that we should regard NISQ devices as 'a significant step toward the more powerful quantum technologies of the future'. Fully fault-tolerant quantum computing, where errors are actively corrected as they occur, remains the ultimate goal. Error correction requires many physical qubits to create a single reliable logical qubit, and we are not yet at the scale where this is practical for general-purpose computing.

WHAT QUANTUM COMPUTERS CAN AND CANNOT DO

It's important to understand both the potential and the limitations of quantum computing. A common misconception is that quantum computers are simply 'faster versions of classical computers'. In reality, they are fundamentally different tools suited to specific kinds of problems.

Quantum computers excel at:

- **optimisation problems:** finding the best solution from enormous numbers of possibilities (route planning, portfolio optimisation);
- **simulation of quantum systems:** modelling molecules and materials for drug discovery and materials science;
- **certain mathematical problems:** factoring large numbers and solving discrete logarithms (which has profound implications for cryptography);
- **machine learning:** potentially accelerating pattern recognition and data analysis.

Quantum computers cannot:

- solve problems that classical computers fundamentally cannot solve;
- provide speedups for everyday tasks like web browsing or document processing;
- replace classical computers for most routine computing needs.

A crucial point is that any problem a quantum computer can solve, a classical computer can also solve given enough time. The promise of quantum computing is not about solving the unsolvable, but about solving certain problems **exponentially faster**, turning calculations that would take millions of years into ones that might take hours or minutes.

QUANTUM TIMELINE

Pre-1980s:

- 1935: Einstein, Podolsky and Rosen propose the EPR paradox, challenging quantum mechanics.

- 1950s–1960s: Richard Feynman and others explore quantum mechanics' potential for computation.

1980s–1990s:

- 1981: Richard Feynman proposes the idea of quantum simulation.
- 1985: David Deutsch formalises the concept of a quantum Turing machine.
- 1994: Peter Shor develops Shor's algorithm for factoring large numbers efficiently.
- 1996: Lov Grover invents Grover's search algorithm, providing quadratic speedup for unstructured search.

2000s:

- 2001: IBM and Stanford demonstrate Shor's algorithm using a seven-qubit system.
- 2007: D-Wave announces the first commercial quantum computer (though its 'quantumness' is debated).

2010s:

- 2011: D-Wave sells the first quantum computer to Lockheed Martin.
- 2019: Google claims quantum supremacy, demonstrating that a quantum computer outperformed a classical one on a specific task.[3]

2020s–present:

- 2021: China's Jiuzhang 2.0 achieves quantum advantage in photonic quantum computing.
- 2022: IBM unveils the Osprey processor with 433 qubits.

---

3 But this has been queried, e.g. Pan et al (2022).

- 2023: Researchers develop quantum error correction advancements, reducing decoherence.
- 2024: First successful entanglement experiment (two-metre separation) by Oxford University.
- 2025: Microsoft announce Majorana 1, the world's first quantum processor powered by so-called 'topological qubits', a form of qubit in what Microsoft (2025) call a topological superconductor or 'topoconductor'.

FURTHER READING

The editor teaches quantum computing at the University of Bath and has provided access to his teaching resources, along with any updates to the book as they occur. These can be found at: https://people.bath.ac.uk/masjhd/QuantumTeaching/

2 QUANTUM TECHNOLOGY OVERVIEW

Josie Woolham and Oli Cox

INTRODUCTION

There are three primary classifications of quantum and quantum-inspired hardware. We can think of these as stepping stones:

- Quantum-inspired methods use classical hardware to tackle problems by exploring the solution space in a manner that is inspired by quantum techniques.
- Quantum annealers use quantum hardware to solve optimisation and sampling problems. We will also cover classical annealers that apply similar techniques using classical hardware.
- Gate-based quantum computers are general-purpose quantum computers that can solve a wide range of problem types.

CLASSICAL 'QUANTUM-INSPIRED' APPROACHES

Quantum-inspired computing comprises a range of approaches used to emulate properties that are exhibited by quantum computers on **classical hardware**. In essence, they attempt to scan the solution space of a problem in a manner that is similar to a quantum computer in order to attempt to find the true global solution.

Classical computers are designed to fetch instructions and execute them sequentially. For example, a sequence of instructions might be to load two numbers from memory, then add them together, then store the result back in memory. These instructions have to be completed one after another; however, some complex tasks like graphics processing require a multitude of instructions to be executed that don't necessarily have to be done in sequence. In fact, it is more efficient if instructions can be executed at the same time or in **parallel**.

Quantum-inspired	Annealers	Gate-based
What is it?		
Quantum-inspired methods use classical hardware, so information is represented by bits rather than qubits. The approach aims to simulate the properties of quantum hardware without the challenges around maintaining superposition. An example of this is using graphics processing units (GPUs) to imitate the parallelism that quantum computers can exhibit.	A type of quantum hardware that initiates a quantum state and allows it to evolve naturally. The nature of this process means that this approach is appropriate for specific types of optimisation and sampling problems only. Note: digital versions are also available that simulate the annealing process.	A general-purpose quantum computer that can run any algorithm that can be represented by a quantum circuit. These computers are referred to as gate-based as they are built to apply quantum gates (akin to logical gates for classical computers) to the quantum state to perform operations.

(Continued)

Quantum-inspired	Annealers	Gate-based
When will it be useful?		
Now – quantum-inspired approaches are not held back by the challenges that quantum hardware faces, so are currently being used to solve problems that previous classical approaches were unable to tackle.	Now, but it's still developing. Annealers are more developed than gate-based quantum computers but are still early technology.	Estimates range anywhere from 5 to 30 years from now.
Pros of the hardware		
Inexpensive to run and easy to integrate into existing architecture. Not dependent on the development of quantum hardware.	Demonstrated improvement on runtimes compared to classical computers for a certain class of problems. Annealers are developing faster than gate-based quantum computers since the error rate is easier to mitigate.	Provides an exponential or polynomial speedup for some problems when compared to classical computers. Additionally, nature itself behaves in a quantum manner, so gate-based hardware allows for more accurate simulations of natural situations such as chemical simulations.

(Continued)

Quantum-inspired	Annealers	Gate-based
	You can repeat the process multiple times as you let a quantum state evolve by changing the landscape. It is less error prone also because it is probabilistic and more heuristic.	
Cons of the hardware		
Quantum algorithms cannot run on classical hardware. So, although more efficient algorithms can be designed for more efficiently designed hardware, this does not tackle the problem of exponential scaling. The rate of improvement is not fast enough to solve many complex computational problems. It is difficult to estimate the resources required to solve problems using this method since it is not heuristic – we don't know how it scales.	Suited for optimisation and sampling problems only.	Gate-based quantum computers are expensive, and there are significant engineering challenges – notably to do with decoherence. As of now, it also usually requires specialist knowledge to write quantum algorithms.

(Continued)

Quantum-inspired	Annealers	Gate-based
What's holding it back?		
As we produce ever smaller chips, we're reaching a point where transistors can't shrink any more. There have historically been issues with supply. The lower range of solvable problems partially holds back industry demand.	While annealers are developing faster than gate-based quantum computers, the lower range of problems they can solve has led many larger hardware developers to focus primarily on gate-based computers.	It is very challenging to reduce noise and prevent decoherence of gate-based computers. It is difficult to construct elaborate entangled states using many qubits. In the current landscape there is no clear 'best approach' to constructing gate-based computers – there are lots of types of qubits. Quantum error correction requires further development.
Use cases		
Lower-complexity problems.	Optimisation and sampling problems.	Optimisation, modelling, factor finding for RSA, quantum search, etc.

For example, a computer game might have two moving objects on the screen at the same time. Instead of calculating the new position of one object then calculating the new position of the second object before updating the screen, calculating the new positions at the same time allows for the screen to be updated twice as fast, meaning better video quality. The demand for better-quality graphics and improved speeds led to the development of GPUs. First used for video games, developers have subsequently used GPUs to tackle other types of programming tasks that can benefit from parallelisation.

One particular use case that has seen demand for GPUs surge is artificial intelligence. Using GPUs instead of classical CPUs allows for more complex machine learning models to be developed that can process larger volumes of data in a reasonable amount of time.

In the context of quantum computing, GPUs can be used to accelerate techniques used to simulate quantum circuits including state vector simulation and tensor networks that rely on matrix operations to emulate quantum operations.

GPUs were also used in 2024 to prove that a 41-million-digit number is a prime number,[1] the largest proven prime number to date. This is significant in the field of number theory and goes to show that the huge parallel speedups offered by GPU technology will allow us to tackle more and more complex problems. While this is hugely impressive, there is still a gap between the capability of GPUs and the potential capability of quantum computers. We will see in later chapters that Shor's algorithm provides an exponential speedup compared to the best-known classical algorithm for another problem in number theory – integer factorisation. This has significant implications for cryptography and digital security.

The other main quantum-inspired approach is a digital annealer, which uses classical hardware to emulate a similar approach to quantum annealers. To understand these, it is

---

1 https://www.mersenne.org/primes/?press=M136279841

best to discuss quantum annealers first, after which we can revisit these digital annealers.

QUANTUM ANNEALERS

The first type of truly quantum hardware we will cover is quantum annealers. They work by setting up a quantum state and then leaving it to evolve **naturally** to obtain the outcome. Annealers use microwave pulses to control the environment around the superposition state to ensure that it evolves meaningfully and to allow it to approach the 'true' solution sought. Because they rely on the natural evolution of states, they can only solve a certain set of problems, namely optimisation and sampling problems.

In order to solve complex problems that correspond to elaborate superposition states, we need a large number of qubits to be able to construct such a state. One might therefore imagine that more qubits automatically means a better quantum computer, but this misses a crucial point.

In fact, the main challenge currently holding back the development of quantum computers pertains to maintaining the superposition state for an extended period of time. The superposition state is extremely sensitive and tends to collapse into one of the base states – that is, our rotating coin will land on heads or tails before we can use it for our computations. We call this phenomenon **decoherence**. This can cause algorithms to fail because, instead of operations being performed on the superposition state, they are performed on the collapsed state, giving unexpected results. There are a number of approaches used to minimise decoherence, which largely consist of isolating the quantum system (primarily through supercooling the system to extremely low temperatures) as well as employing quantum error correction methods.

Another limitation can arise from limited connectivity between qubits. Hardware constraints, particularly in annealers, can limit the number of neighbours that each qubit can couple to. A common workaround for this is to use clusters of qubits to encode each logical variable, although this results in us needing more qubits than the problem would initially suggest.

An advantage that quantum annealers have over gate-based computers is that they don't manipulate the fragile quantum superposition state, which means that they are less severely hampered by decoherence. This has allowed manufacturers of quantum annealers, spearheaded by companies such as D-Wave or NEC, to be able to develop their hardware more rapidly than their gate-based counterparts so far. Having said this, they still remain some way from solving many full-scale real-world problems, and since they are still affected by decoherence, there are a few error correction procedures that exist for annealers, including quantum annealing correction (QAC; Pudenz et al., 2014).

At of the time of publishing, the most prominent approach for quantum annealers comes from the American firm D-Wave,[2] which involves initialising qubits in a superposition state and then altering the probabilities so that, by the end of the annealing process, the qubits have the highest probability of collapsing into a classical state that corresponds to an optimal solution. The quantum annealer also uses a device called a **coupler** to achieve entanglement across multiple qubits. Each qubit has its own magnetic field, and probabilities can be altered by applying an external magnetic field to the qubits. The external magnetic field is controlled by the **bias** term in the quantum algorithm.

While the spotlight has been on quantum annealers in recent times, annealing was actually originally developed as a classical method (Kirkpatrick et al., 1983). As such, there are also a number of classical annealers that don't have the innate complexities that come with the quantum hardware, such as decoherence (and the supercooling that's then required). These classical annealers are becoming increasingly popular in industry since quantum annealers are still some way off for several problems; however, since they are not actually quantum (we would also call them 'quantum-inspired'), they

2 docs.dwavequantum.com/en/latest/quantum_research/quantum_annealing_intro.html

are often not able to replicate the speed or efficiency of their quantum counterparts.

Simulated annealers run on general purpose classical hardware (CPUs and GPUs) while digital annealers are typically built using specialised hardware that emulates quantum technology.

For example, Fujitsu's Digital Annealer emulates quantum computing by partitioning the system in order to run multiple problems in parallel when required, without the need for supercooling and advanced isolation techniques.

GATE-BASED QUANTUM COMPUTERS

While quantum annealers rely on natural evolution of the superposition state, gate-based quantum computers can actively control and manipulate the state using quantum gates. This unlocks a wider range of problems that they can solve; in fact, a gate-based quantum computer can be configured to run any quantum circuit, while the same cannot be said for annealers.

However, since we are now manipulating the highly sensitive quantum state, this also means that the system is far more sensitive and error prone.

As well as supercooling the quantum computers, error correction methods are applied to mitigate the effects of decoherence and noise. These error correction techniques are essential for creating a useful quantum computer, but also require dedicated error-correcting qubits.

One example of an error-correcting method is **majority voting**. This method involves running the quantum circuit multiple times and taking the solution that is produced the most frequently as the correct solution. For example, we might have a quantum circuit that should run to produce the output 1. However, due to the inherent uncertainty of quantum computers, there might be a chance that it outputs 0. If we simply run the circuit three times and measure 0, 1 and 1, we would take 1 to be the correct solution since it is the majority answer. This reduces the likelihood of getting the wrong answer, although it takes three times the number of physical qubits, and it also must be applied at the end of the algorithm (an important distinction from classical majority voting). In reality, more efficient error-correcting methods are being used and developed – quantum error correction is a crucial and fast-developing field.

Physical qubits can be constructed by various methods, and different qubit technologies have different processing speeds and levels of stability. Companies such as IBM and Google have developed quantum computers using **superconducting** qubits, which are made from loops of superconducting material. One example is Google's Sycamore processor, which was the first device to make a serious claim[3] to **quantum supremacy** – the principle of demonstrating that a quantum computer can complete a task in a reasonable amount of time, while no classical computer could complete the same task in a reasonable amount of time.

Other approaches include using trapped-ion qubits made of individual, charged atoms – developed, for example, by companies such as IonQ and Honeywell. Scientists have been able to use electromagnetic fields to control these qubits effectively, although since the ions all have the same charge they repel each other, making this approach challenging to scale up. Neutral atoms are another approach (being developed by companies such as QuEra) that is attempting to sidestep this issue.[4]

A number of other approaches exist, including photonic qubits, spin qubits and more. While different companies are placing their bets on certain approaches over others, we are yet to see which approaches will emerge above others – in the current landscape these different approaches are each more or less suited to specific problem sets.

---

3 But this has been queried, e.g. Pan et al. (2022).

4 quantamagazine.org/the-best-qubits-for-quantum-computing-might-just-be-atoms-20240325/

3 QUANTUM COMPUTING PRINCIPLES

Marco Ugo Gambetta

INTRODUCTION

In this chapter we aim to understand the journey of a quantum algorithm.

Classical information theory encodes information in binary form (0 and 1) and manipulates such information through a series of logical gates. For example, the NOT gate flips a bit from 0 to 1 and vice versa, and it is completely deterministic, so a user always knows the output of the computation. The information is stored in classical bits that are usually transistors.

With quantum computing, on the other hand, the user would like to apply the same binary methodology to quantum systems (e.g., superconducting material, ions, photons) so that they can take advantage of some quantum phenomena like superposition and entanglement during the computation and manipulation of the information. At this stage, the story becomes more interesting, as quantum objects live in an intrinsically probabilistic world. When the information is encoded as quantum states, we can apply some operations that are going to create unusual behaviours. For example, we can create a quantum state that is simultaneously '0' and '1' (superposition), or we can couple qubits (quantum bits) of information so that they are extremely correlated (entanglement). Each qubit behaves in a probabilistic fashion, but as a pair they behave deterministically (in the sense that the probabilistic behaviour of one is 100% correlated with the behaviour of the other).

We can understand this concept with the famous example of Schrödinger's cat. The cat is closed in a box together with a radioactive isotope that has a probability of 50% of decaying in a fixed amount of time (say one hour); if the decay is detected then a flask of poison in the box is broken, killing the cat. We can imagine the box as the quantum world and the cat and the isotope as two quantum information carriers that are now entangled. The Copenhagen interpretation of quantum mechanics states that the cat is **both** dead **and** alive as long as the box remains closed, and it will be **either** dead **or** alive as soon as we open the box, i.e., perform the measurement (open the gate from quantum to classical). Now the cat is in a superposition because, while the box is closed, the cat can be dead and alive, presenting a probabilistic behaviour, **but** it is deterministically linked to the isotope as only two possible outcomes are possible: dead cat + decayed isotope or alive cat + not decayed isotope.

How can we use these behaviours to achieve some sort of practical advantage?

The idea behind a quantum algorithm is usually the following:

1. Encode all the possible inputs as a superposition (often referred to as parallel computing).
2. Apply our algorithm to try to increase the probability of measuring the input that provides the desired output (the solution that we are looking for).
3. Measure with higher probability the solution we are interested in.

Physically, this means tweaking the uniformity of the superposition by using the wave behaviour of quantum objects with constructive and destructive interference. Algorithmically, we need to identify a unitary matrix able to perform a rotation (computation) of the starting input. The theoretical goal is then to apply a series of unitary matrices and to measure with the correct basis. Last, but not least, from a practical perspective we need to apply a series of quantum gates that approximate the target matrix, apply a series of gates to perform the base translation, and measure with the engineering instruments that are available.

The whole game is then to understand how to manipulate the information so that we achieve the desired result.

QUANTUM ALGORITHMS

Classical data needs to be encoded and there are two main methods to do so: through amplitude encoding and through a more standard encoding. Standard encoding assigns the bit of information to a single qubit, therefore 0 will become $|0\rangle$ and 1 will become $|1\rangle$.[1] Now, the interesting thing is that in order to encode the possibility of both values, we only need one qubit as we can store both outputs by creating a superposition of the two, $(|0\rangle + |1\rangle)/\sqrt{2}$, where the $1/\sqrt{2}$ is a normalisation factor, known as the amplitude, that describes the probability of a certain outcome to be measured with respect to the computational basis. The probability is given by squaring the amplitude, in our case $[(|0\rangle + |1\rangle)/\sqrt{2}]^2 = 1/2 = 50\%$ probability, i.e., uniform superposition.

On the other hand, amplitude encoding encodes the data as the amplitude (the probability of being measured) of each input, working somehow as random-access memory, so that if you have *n* data points, you can store those (once normalised) as the probability of each qubit. This technique is used, for example, in the Harrow–Hassidim–Lloyd (HHL) algorithm. The disadvantage of this technique is that you do not have access to the data once it is encoded, even though you can retrieve it through quantum amplitude estimation. Depending on the quantum algorithm routine that you need to perform, you might want to use one or the other type of encoding.

The power of quantum can already be grasped at this stage, as quantum systems allow the encoding of exponentially

1 See Chapter 4 for more on this notation.

more information than classical systems; however, if we do not apply clever algorithms, the answer that will be read will be completely random. These limitations are mathematically represented by Heisenberg's uncertainty principle and the Holevo bound.

Once the data is encoded, the user can start applying 'gates' that together represent a given unitary matrix (i.e., an operation that can be reversed). The information manipulation is where the user can apply algorithms like HHL, Grover, Shor, or others to use the full power of quantum effects to obtain the desired result.

Once the quantum system has evolved to the desired state, the user needs to read out the solution, and that step is called **measurement**. A very important concept is that measurement is the only way to access the information encoded in quantum states, and once the measurement is performed, the quantum state will be corrupted; therefore, it is the only operation that cannot be reversed.

This is the journey for simple algorithms assuming access to computers with logical (error-free) qubits, but quantum implementations cannot be considered error free. Error is always present, even in classical computers, and in quantum it is even more relevant as quantum objects can be easily disturbed by very small changes in temperature, electromagnetic fields, and so on. For this reason, many quantum computing systems are shielded and cooled almost to 0°K.

That is why error correction subroutines may be implemented throughout the code; these use ancillary qubits to check the condition of the overall state. Oversimplifying, one can couple a target qubit with an ancillary qubit in order to see if the target is spoiled (if we have a Geiger counter, we can assume that no signal means a live cat).

For this reason, NISQ (noisy intermediate-scale quantum) algorithms are looking into the error robustness of the subroutines, because with a higher tolerance to error, we can spend fewer resources in correcting the qubits.

As we learned from the theoretical routine, we need to perform gate composition (recreate the algorithm with a physical implementation that is feasible to engineer) and measure. The next step is to perform the routine on an actual piece of hardware; depending on the topology, certain operations will be more/less reliable. For example, with superconducting qubits we can quickly manipulate single qubits, but two-qubit interactions are less reliable (low fidelity), while with ions, operations are more reliable but are slower. On the other hand, in photonic quantum computers it is easy to entangle and allow large systems of qubits to interact, but it is hard to control a single photon.[2] In a nutshell, every system has pros and cons, and the constitution of the algorithm needs to take this factor into consideration at this stage.

The most recognised performance indicators for a quantum algorithm are circuit width (how many qubits do I need?) and circuit depth (how many sequential operations do I need?), but more metrics are emerging – e.g., CLOPS (circuit layer operations per second; how fast is the algorithm?) and the number of two-qubit gates (how many CNOTs?), since they are the most error prone for now.

Application

We have now seen the basic building blocks (qubits), basic operations (gates), and basic readouts (measurements), and discussed error, architectures, and encoding, but how can we take advantage of all this?

Let's consider a very famous algorithm for unstructured database search: Grover's algorithm. The assumption is that we need to find a specific input in a puzzle and that this input is the result of some logical (mathematical) operation, e.g., find the result of a Sudoku.

2 See Chapter 5 for details of these different architectures.

In a nutshell, the algorithm works like this:[3]

1. It creates a uniform superposition: it stores together all possible inputs or combinations in a fixed number of qubits.
2. It performs inversion by the mean, i.e., uses a 'quantum oracle' to amplify through the interference the solution that solves the problem.
3. It performs the measurement to retrieve the solution.

What is a quantum oracle? It is a function that in this specific case changes the phase to the input that solves the puzzle, the answer to our Sudoku. One might ask, if we have a function that can flag the right answer, why don't we just use that without the overhead? The answer is because it is easier to encode a set of rules and 'check' the solution rather than find a new one from scratch. If someone hands you a filled Sudoku you can almost instantly tell whether it is wrong or right, but finding the solution to a blank Sudoku will require more time. For more information on this subject, called complexity theory, we suggest looking into 'P vs. NP', which is also one of the seven Millennium Problems in mathematics. If you solve this, you can win $1 million!

Grover's algorithm provides quadratic speedup, i.e., it is quadratically better than the best-known algorithm for unstructured database search. Algorithm speedup is almost always considered against the best-known equivalent algorithm, as it is very challenging to provide a minimum threshold for a certain problem. How can you prove that the best strategy requires exactly x resources (steps) with respect to the input? What if there is a very weird strategy that requires only $x/2$ or $\log x$? In some cases there exist lower bounds that are mathematically proven, but in other cases, especially for real-life applications, it is enough to find something that works better.

---

3 See Chapter 4 for a more detailed look at this and other quantum algorithms.

Interest in quantum computers also appeared because the speedup of some algorithms is exponential, like Shor's algorithm and HHL. Shor's algorithm uses quantum fast Fourier transforms to find the period of a number, which can be used to solve problems like the factorisation problem (the basis for the RSA cypher and its descendants that are widely used in internet cybersecurity) and the discrete logarithm problem (the basis for other widely used encryption systems for internet cybersecurity). HHL is an algorithm that solves systems of linear equations exponentially faster.

The three algorithms presented in this chapter provide theoretical advantages but still have hardware and algorithmic difficulties that the quantum community needs to address in order to apply them in real-life applications. If we consider Grover, one of the algorithmic difficulties is how to build the oracle; in HHL, we can find the solution to the system of linear equations as a quantum state, but how do we retrieve the solution?

Quantum computers have enormous potential to solve important problems efficiently, and the community is working hard to find solutions to these problems. The take-home message that we would like to convey is that this is a new paradigm of computation, and it requires some changes to how we think of algorithms. A competitive advantage can be obtained by understanding the basic concepts in the early stages of the process.

4 QUANTUM ALGORITHMS

James Davenport and Jessica Jones

INTRODUCTION

There are two major computation models for true quantum computing: the adiabatic model (very roughly analogous to analogue computing) and the qubit/gate model (roughly analogous to digital computing).

ADIABATIC QUANTUM COMPUTING

Adiabatic quantum computing is the theory underpinning quantum annealing. It is not discussed as much as the gate model (see later in this chapter), but is arguably currently more useful. In theory (and hence assuming error-free computation, which is a big assumption at the moment), the two models are polynomial-time equivalent (Aharonov et al., 2004).

The key concept is that of the **Hamiltonian**, generally denoted H, of a quantum system. From our point of view, we can regard this as something quantum physicists understand and we don't need to. The 'ground state' of a Hamiltonian is the state of minimal energy of that system. The physicists have produced a useful theorem.

Theorem 4.1 (Quantum adiabatic theorem). *If we have a time-varying Hamiltonian, $H(t)$, whose initial state is H_I at time $t = 0$ and whose final state is H_F at some later time $t = t_F$, then if the system is initially in the ground state of H_I, and as long as the time evolution of the Hamiltonian is sufficiently slow, the state is likely to remain in the ground state throughout the evolution, therefore being in the ground state of H_F at time $t = t_F$.*

To use this, we let H_I be some Hamiltonian whose ground state is easy to prepare, and H_F be a Hamiltonian whose ground state is what we are looking for, generally the minimum of some system. Then we choose some function $s(t)$, known as an **adiabatic evolution path**, such that $s(0) = 1$ and $s(t_F) = 0$. Then we let our Hamiltonian be

$$H(t) = s(t)H_I + (1 - s(t))H_F, \tag{4.1}$$

so that $H(0) = H_I$ and $H(t_F) = H_F$. A common choice is the linear function $s(t) = (1 - t/t_F)$. t_F is chosen so that the evolution is 'sufficiently slow', and again we have to ask the physicists what this means.

QUANTUM ANNEALING

'Annealing' is a process in metallurgy where a metal is heated above its crystallisation temperature, so that atoms can migrate and dislocations be remedied, and then cooled, hopefully getting a more ductile and workable piece of metal. By dint of a major leap of imagination, computer scientists have invented the algorithm paradigm 'simulated annealing'[1] for optimisation, where we start exploring the surface we wish to minimise 'hot', i.e. prepared to accept larger values, and gradually become 'cooler', i.e. less likely to accept larger values.

A further leap of imagination takes us to quantum annealing, which is an application of quantum adiabatic computing to optimisation. Here we let H_F be the Hamiltonian of correct solutions, whose ground state is therefore a minimum correct solution. Let H_D be some other Hamiltonian which does not commute with H_F, i.e. $H_F H_D \neq H_D H_F$. Let $\Gamma(t)$ be what is called the **transverse field coefficient**, which we can think of as the simulated temperature in the annealing analogy – it is going to start very high and reduce to zero over time. Then, instead of (4.1), we have this Hamiltonian:

1 The name is due to Kirkpatrick et al. (1983).

$$H(t) = \Gamma(t)H_D + H_F. \tag{4.2}$$

Initially H_D dominates, and the system is in all sorts of states. As $\Gamma(t)$ decreases, the energy ends up in the ground state (of a combination of temperatures T_D and T_F), and by Theorem 4.1 it should stay in a ground state until $\Gamma(t) = 0$ and $H(t) = H_F$, at which point we can read off the solution, which should be the minimum.

Implementations

In 2011, the Californian company D-Wave Systems announced the first commercial quantum annealer on the market, called D-Wave One (Johnson et al., 2011). The problem that is natively solved by the D-Wave machines is known to physicists as an Ising spin glass model, and the Hamiltonian is

$$\sum_{i=1}^{n} h_i\sigma_i^z + \sum_{i=1}^{n-1}\sum_{j=i+1}^{n} J_{i,j}\sigma_i^z\sigma_j^z, \tag{4.3}$$

where (as stated after Venegas-Andraca et al. (2018, (4)), which goes into much more detail over the physics) σ_i^z is the Pauli matrix z acting on particle i, h_i is the magnetic field on particle i and $J_{i,j}$ is the coupling strength between particles i and j.

A computer scientist would regard (4.3) as an instance of a QUBO (quadratic unconstrained Boolean optimisation) problem, and write it as

$$\sum_{i=1}^{n} p_i x_i + \sum_{i=1}^{n-1}\sum_{j=i+1}^{n} q_{i,j}x_i x_j \tag{4.4}$$

where the x_i are now Boolean variables. The computer scientist classes QUBO as an NP-hard problem, meaning that many difficult problems, such as the travelling salesman, can be converted into QUBO problems. There is a set of problems readily convertible into QUBO in Lucas (2014), with important extensions and corrections in Lodewijks (2019).

Current status

In recent years, small- and intermediate-scale quantum processors that implement quantum annealing have begun to become available. Although noisy and so far without error correction, these can provide on the order of 1000 physical qubits, and thus problems amenable to quantum annealing have begun to be adapted for these machines. Currently, only very small, 'toy' problems are practical, and a hybrid approach, as described in Esposito et al. (2023), is generally accepted as necessary for the medium term.

Use cases

A number of combinatorial optimisation problems can be reconstructed as quantum annealing problems and thus be rendered amenable, potentially, to being solved on suitable quantum hardware. The details are presented in the following boxes for the interested reader.

SATISFIABILITY SOLVING

Satisfiability, henceforth referred to as SAT, refers to the property of a Boolean formula to be 'satisfied', that is, true under a specific assignment of its input variables. There may be more than one assignment under which the formula can be said to be satisfiable. SAT solvers such as MiniSAT (Eén and Sörensson, 2003) are computer programs that attempt to find one or more of these assignments, and take as input a set of constraints.

This makes them ideal for searching for an optimal (not necessarily the unique optimal) solution to questions that can be formulated as a set of constraints to be satisfied. In particular, there are D-Wave routines for this.[a] In principle, any problem that can be restated as a SAT problem can also be reformulated as a quantum annealing problem instead.

a docs.dwavequantum.com/en/latest/quantum_research/example_sat_unconstrained.html

SUPEROPTIMISATION

Although SAT solvers in general perform very well and can give very good results, some problems are too large (have too many constraints) to run on classical hardware. For example, superoptimisation[b] using SAT, such as in TOAST (Brain et al., 2006), has had to target small hotspots of application code rather than being applied to the entire application, even for fairly simple programs. As we get better quantum computers, we can hope that the range of superoptimisation will grow.

---

b Producing the best possible machine code, rather than just good machine code.

LARGE-SCALE TELECOMMUNICATIONS NETWORK DESIGN

As well as the well-known travelling salesman problem, combinatorial optimisation problems include many real-world problems such as network traffic flow optimisation, required, for example, for telecommunications network planning. This has used a number of approaches, including SAT and genetic algorithms, to optimise for small areas (Calégari et al., 2001). However, with much larger areas and more radio bands to consider, including satellite cover as well as base transceiver stations, it is proving difficult to model on a large enough scale: 5G, using a different part of the spectrum from 4G, has different requirements for tower placement; as the short wavelengths utilised for these types of communication are generally line-of-sight, obstructions such as hills and buildings must be taken into account; propagation can even be affected by the make-up of the landscape rather than simply its shape – whether it is sand or clay, or features large bodies of water.

MAX-CUT

Maximum cut, also referred to as max-cut, is the problem of how best to partition a graph into two sub-graphs such that the weights of the edges of the graph spanning the cut between the two sub-graphs is maximised (weighted max-cut). It can, in an unweighted graph, simply maximise the number of edges that must be cut in order to separate the two subgraphs from one another. This problem is known to be NP-hard, and as such cannot be solved in polynomial time on classical hardware (unless P = NP). It is also APX-hard, so there are no arbitrarily good polynomial-time approximation algorithms that can be applied to this problem either. However, the max-cut problem can be reduced to the Ising model (Barahona et al., 1988), and is hence suitable for quantum annealing.

We do not have to use the specialised hardware needed for quantum annealing. There is an alternative algorithm – the quantum approximate optimisation algorithm (QAOA) – that runs on the 'standard' gate model computer. However, quantum annealing (Kadowaki and Nishimori, 1998) seems to be a better-performing alternative (Pelofske et al., 2024) to QAOA (Farhi et al., 2014; Hadfield et al., 2019; Cook et al., 2020). See also the work on max-cut on a hybrid quantum–classical system (Esposito et al., 2023; Esposito and Danzig, 2024).

QUANTUM MACHINE LEARNING

It will not have escaped the observant that max-cut can be considered a binary classification model. In simple terms, binary classification takes a collection of things or data points and separates them into two groups. For example, spam or not spam in the case of email, or whether or not an image contains a face. It is one of the foundations of machine learning and applicable to a wide variety of areas. Many of these problems can be reformulated for quantum hardware. However, Hoefler et al. (2023, table 1) point out that even an 'optimistic' quantum computer has far less I/O bandwidth than a classical computer. To quote from that article, 'generally, quantum computers will be practical for "*big compute*" *problems on small data*, not big data problems'.

QUBIT ALGORITHMS IN THE GATE MODEL

For these algorithms, we assume that we have a supply of quantum bits (qubits), each of which can be in a superposition of two basis states, which are generally called $|0\rangle$ and $|1\rangle$,[2] with 'probability amplitudes' α and β, which are complex numbers (hence the quotation marks round 'probability amplitudes') such that, if we measure the qubit $\alpha|0\rangle + \beta|1\rangle$, we will get $|0\rangle$ with probability $|\alpha|^2$ and $|1\rangle$ with probability $|\beta|^2$. In particular, the qubit $h := (|0\rangle + |1\rangle)/\sqrt{2}$ represents '$|0\rangle$ and $|1\rangle$ with equal probability': a quantum value that has no classical equivalent. The Hadamard gate **H** is a basic quantum circuit that converts $|0\rangle$ into h, and $|1\rangle$ into $h' := (|0\rangle - |1\rangle)/\sqrt{2}$.

Note that the choice of which 'directions' are $|0\rangle$ and $|1\rangle$ is arbitrary (but they must be at right angles), so the Hadamard basis h and h' would be a valid alternative. But we have to be consistent: if we have $|0\rangle$, but measure it in the Hadamard basis, we have a 50% chance of getting h and a 50% chance of getting h' (and vice versa). This is key to the various quantum key distribution ideas (see later in this chapter).

The general language for describing quantum programs, the rough equivalent of pseudocode, is the quantum circuit, as shown in Figures 4.1–4.3. The full notation is quite complex, but for our purposes it is sufficient to note that each qubit, or set of n qubits (denoted $\underline{\;/n\;}$), is a horizontal rail

2 $|0\rangle$ and $|1\rangle$ are examples of the **Dirac notation** (Dirac, 1939), which is widespread in quantum mechanics. For the purposes of this chapter, it suffices to regard them as abstract symbols.

running through the circuit, with boxes indicating the various quantum operations. The exponent $\otimes n$ means 'n copies of'. In particular, the measurement operator denotes a measurement operation.[3] We will use $\oplus$ to represent binary addition, so $1 \oplus 1 = 0$.

The Deutsch–Jozsa algorithm

The Deutsch–Jozsa algorithm (Deutsch and Jozsa, 1992) is a brilliant example of the theoretical power of quantum computing. Suppose that we have a function f from n bits to a single bit, **and** we are guaranteed that **either** f is constant (always returns the same value) **or** f is balanced, i.e. for half the possible values we get 0, and for the other half, we get 1. The only conventional method is to try enough values. If we get both 0 and 1, we know the function is balanced, but to be sure it is constant, we need to get the same value for $2^{n-1} + 1$ values. The Deutsch–Jozsa algorithm does the same in **one** quantum evaluation (but at a superposition of all possible inputs).

DEUTSCH–JOZSA DETAILS

The Deutsch–Jozsa algorithm assumes we have a 'quantum oracle' U_f for f, i.e. a circuit that represents f. More precisely, it takes n qubits representing x and one more qubit y, and outputs[c] x and $y \oplus f(x)$. This oracle is used in the circuit shown in Figure 4.1. First we apply Hadamard gates H to the input, so that x is a superposition of all possible n-bit strings, and y is a superposition of $|0\rangle$ and $|1\rangle$. This is what we see as $|\psi_1\rangle$. We then apply the 'oracle' U_f.

c The reader may ask why it outputs x. The answer is that every quantum circuit has to be reversible (because it's equivalent to a unitary matrix in Hilbert space), and knowing x means that we can compute $f(x)$, and can reverse from $y \oplus f(x)$ to y.

3 Measurement symbol by Geek3, CC BY 3.0, commons.wikimedia.org/w/index.php?curid=45450138.

Figure 4.1 Deutsch–Jozsa circuit (By Peplm, CC BY-SA 4.0, commons.wikimedia.org/w/index.php?curid=75740173)

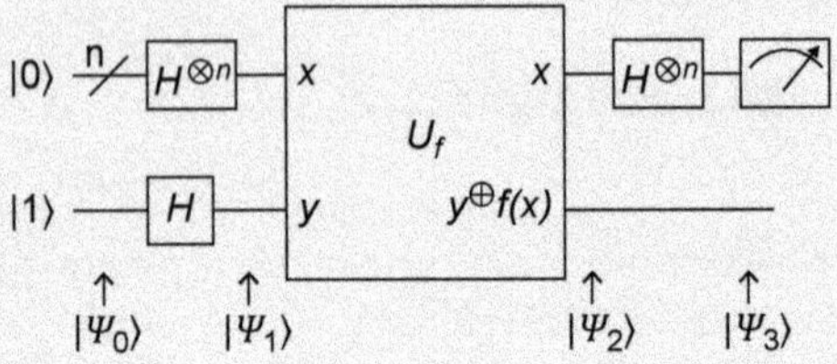

Although we stated that U_f doesn't change x, a phenomenon known as 'phase kickback' means that the x component is in fact $(-1)^f(x)x$. We then transform this back by applying **H** to each qubit in x. After this, if f is constant we measure $|0\rangle$ with probability 1, and if f is balanced we get $|1\rangle$ with probability 1. Note that if f is neither, we get either $|0\rangle$ or $|1\rangle$ with some probability depending on how close f is to being balanced.

Figure 4.2 Grover's algorithm (By Fawly, CC BY-SA 4.0, commons.wikimedia.org/w/index.php?curid=106362482)

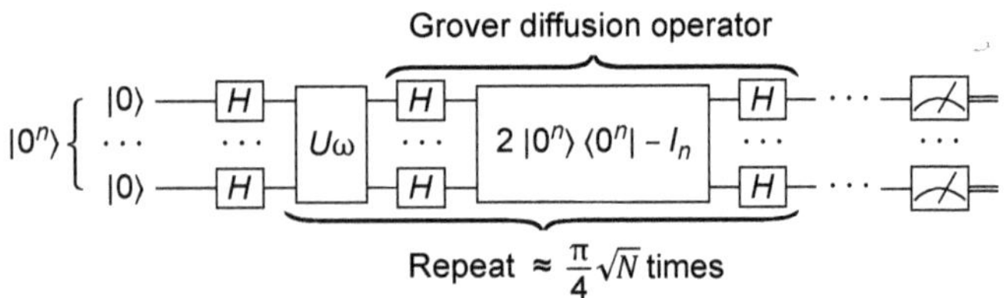

Grover's algorithm

Grover's algorithm is described in Grover (1996), but note that the title 'A fast quantum mechanical algorithm for database search' is misleading: we don't use it for databases, as that would imply encoding the entire database as a quantum circuit. The practical uses of Grover's algorithm are when we have a function f from n bits to a single bit, and we want to find the unique value w of those n bits that gives us 1, rather than 0. A typical f might be 'does this n-bit string hash to a certain value', as in reversing cryptographic password hashing. If f is a strong hashing function, then the only conventional method is to try all possible $N = 2^n$ values until we find the right one, with an average running time of $N/2 = 2^{n-1}$ tests.

Basic Grover

Grover's algorithm assumes f is given by means of an operator U_w such that

$$U_w x = \begin{cases} -x & \text{when } x = w, \text{ i.e. } f(x) = 1, \\ x & \text{when } x \neq w, \text{ i.e. } f(x) = 0 \end{cases}$$

(again, this operator is reversible). This operator reflects the w component of an arbitrary state. The other operator Grover's algorithm needs is the diffusion operator U_s, which reflects about the uniform superposition. Since the uniform superposition is the result of applying **H** to $|0\rangle$ **and vice versa**, we can compute U_s by **H**, then reflect about 0 (i.e. U_0), then another **H** to undo the first. The combination $U_w U_s$ increases the amplitude of w by roughly $1/\sqrt{N}$. Hence, if we repeat the operation $\pi\sqrt{N}/4$ times, the probability of measuring the correct w is almost 1 ($1 - O(1/N)$, to be more precise).

This gives us the circuit shown in Figure 4.2. A fuller geometric interpretation is given in many sources, e.g. Wikipedia or Microsoft Learn.[4]

4 learn.microsoft.com/en-us/azure/quantum/concepts-grovers

Observation 4.1. Note that the diagram implies roughly $\pi\sqrt{N}/4$ replications of the $U_w U_s$ block. In a classical programming system, we wouldn't write out the line(s) of code many times, we would have a loop. But there is no such construct in quantum programming: we do need to repeat the circuit block.

Multiple values

So far we have assumed that there is a unique *w*. If there are precisely two such *w*s, then in fact the same argument applies with $N/2$ in place of N – we repeat the Grover iteration $\pi\sqrt{N/2}/4$ times, and have a high probability of getting one of the *w*s (but we have no control over which). Similarly, if we know there are three *w* values, and so on.

UNKNOWN MULTIPLE

But what if we just knew that there are *k*, somewhere between one and five, values of *w*. The classical programmer would proceed as follows:

1. Set up Grover.
2. Repeat the iteration $\pi\sqrt{N/5}/4$ times.
3. See if we have a solution, which we should have if $k = 5$.
4. If not, do a further $\pi(\sqrt{N/4} - \sqrt{N/5})/4$ times.
5. See if we have a solution, which we should have if $k = 4$.
6. ...

But this doesn't work: the 'see if' at step 3 destroys the quantum state in the process of inspecting it. Put another way, 'further' doesn't work!

The correct solution is first to try for N values (i.e. $\lceil\pi/4\rceil = 1$ iterations), then $N/2$ values, then $N/4$ values, ..., then one value. This doesn't cover all possible values, but in practice if there are three values, the runs for four and for two values are very likely to find one of the three.

Grover's algorithm is usually deployed to invert functions, i.e. to find a/the w such that $f(w) = x$. In hashing theory, this is known as the **pre-image** problem. A related problem in hashing theory is the **collision** problem: finding w_1, w_2 such that $f(w_1) = f(w_2)$, without caring what that value is. If f takes n-bit values, and $N = 2^n$ is the number of possible values, the classical pre-image problem takes $O(N)$, and Grover reduces this to $O(\sqrt{N})$. Conversely, the classical collision problem takes $O(\sqrt{N})$ operations, and Brassard et al. (1998) gives a quantum attack that reduces this to $O(\sqrt[3]{N})$ operations.

Grover in practice

An argument that the first author used to hear quite often goes roughly like this.

1. We have exaflop machines, capable of doing 10^{18} calculations per second.
2. Breaking the common code AES-128 requires checking 2^{128} key values, i.e. $2^{128} \approx 256 \times 10^{36}$ operations.
3. But Grover puts a square root in this, so we are looking at 16×10^{18} quantum operations.
4. Hence we ought to be very afraid that a quantum machine could break AES-128 in 16 seconds.

There are various flaws in this argument, of which the most fundamental is the first.

- We do not have exaflop single computers, rather the 'exaflop computers' are, roughly, 10^9 engines each doing 10^9 computations/second, or one per nanosecond. If we assume the same parallelism (10^9 engines) is available with quantum computers, each engine would need to search 256×10^{27} possible key values, which, with the benefit of the 'Grover square root', is 5.06×10^{14} nanoseconds, or six days.
- An AES quantum circuit is an extremely complex object, and we need one such in each U_w; by Observation 4.1 there are roughly 2^{64} such. In fact, Davenport and Pring

(2021) estimated that they would need, after various optimisations, $2^{82.26} \approx 6 \times 10^{24}$ quantum gates for AES-128.

- A one-nanosecond cycle time for error-corrected quantum is extremely optimistic: the current technology for an **error-corrected** quantum operation is measured in microseconds (Brierley, 2025, minute 8:03).

A similar conclusion of infeasibility was reached in Gilkolaei and Ebrahimi (2025). They looked at a cut-down version of the Keccak hash function (full Keccak is standardised as SHA-3). The full version is believed to have complexity 2^{256}, but the three-round version apparently[5] has a classical solution with complexity $2^{57.8}$. Hence, Gilkolaei and Ebrahimi (2025) asked whether Grover's algorithm could give a solution with complexity $\sqrt{2^{57.8}} = 2^{28.9}$. They deduced that in theory it could, but in practice this was infeasible because it would need:

- 3,200 logical qubits;
- and hence (with current technology) 3,200,000 physical qubits (which they describe as 'prohibitive');
- 7.47×10^{13} quantum gates (again, Observation 4.1 applies);
- 43 days on very optimistic machine assumptions (50 ns cycle time) or 2,365 years on more realistic assumptions.

Figure 4.3 Quantum phase of Shor's algorithm (By Bender2k14, CC BY-SA 4.0, commons.wikimedia.org/w/index.php?curid=34319883)

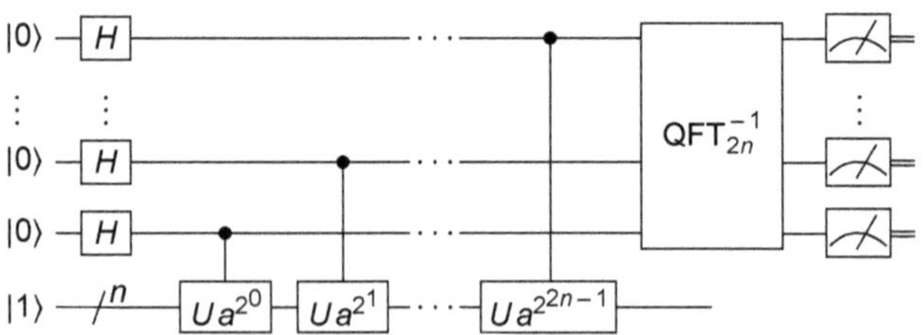

5 But the reference doesn't resolve.

Shor's integer factoring algorithm

For full details, see Shor (1994a, 1994b); we are using a presentation based on Kitaev (1995). Let us assume that N is the number to be factored and it has n bits, i.e. $2^{n-1} \leq N < 2^n$. The algorithm is actually a combination of three phases:

1. classical pre-processing;
2. the quantum phase;
3. classical post-processing, which relies on technical number theory calculations, but is computationally cheap.

Let us look first at the quantum phase.

The quantum phase

This takes as input a classical number N (assumed not to be a prime or a perfect power) and a classical number a, assumed to be relatively prime to N. Let r be the (currently unknown) order of a modulo N, i.e. the least $r > 0$ such that $a^r \pmod N = 1$.

Then the algorithm should output a number of the form (an integer approximation to) $(j/r)2^n$. How do we do this? Essentially the idea is to consider all powers of a in superposition. More precisely, let U_a be the $n \times n$ unitary matrix that corresponds to multiplication by $a \pmod N$, i.e.

$$U_a|k\rangle = \begin{cases} |ak \pmod N\rangle & 0 \leq k < N, \\ \text{as it works out} & N \leq k < 2^n. \end{cases}$$

Because $\gcd(a, N) = 1$, multiplication by a is a permutation of the numbers $0 \leq k < N$, and hence U is unitary. We send a $3n$ qubit into our machine, defined as $|0\rangle^{\otimes 2n} \otimes |1\rangle$, where $|1\rangle$ is an n-bit representation of 1. The machine is shown in Figure 4.3. By the definition of r, $U_a^r = I$, and so the eigenvalues of U_1 are the rth roots of unity, i.e. the powers of $\omega = e^{2\pi i/r}$. The eigenvector corresponding to ω^j is $|\psi_j\rangle = (1/\sqrt{r})\sum_{k=0}^{r-1} \omega^{-kj}|a^k\rangle$. Furthermore, $(1/\sqrt{r})\sum_{j=0}^{r-1} |\psi_j\rangle = |1\rangle$.

It is a property of the inverse quantum Fourier transform (written QFT^{-1}) that the output registers (corresponding to $|0\rangle^{\otimes 2n}$) are all the eigenvalues (scaled by 2^{2n}) in superposition, so when we measure it we get, at random, the nearest integer to some $2^{2n} j/r$.

Classical pre-processing

This is straightforward:

1. Check that N is not prime (Miller–Rabin; Rabin, 1980) – if it is, we are not dealing with RSA.
2. Check that N is not a perfect square, or cube, or ..., or nth power (if it is, we've factored N).
3. Choose a random a and check that $\gcd(a, N) = 1$ (if not, we've already found a factor of N).

Then pass (N, a) to the quantum phase.

Classical post-processing

Let J be the output of the quantum measurement (hopefully $2^{2n} j/r$). If we apply the continued fraction algorithm to J and 2^r, we will recover the fraction j/r, or more precisely $b_1/c_1 = j/r$. We might hope that $c_1 = r$, but there may have been a common factor between j and r, which cancelled in b_1/c_1. Hence we run the quantum phase again, also computing $b_2/c_2 = j_2/r$, where j_2 is the index of the eigenvalue found on the second attempt, and so on. Then our guess at r is lcm $(c_1, c_2, ...)$ (in practice three c_i should suffice).

So now we know that

$$a^r \equiv 1 \pmod{N}. \tag{4.5}$$

If r is even then $(a^{r/2}-1)(a^{r/2}+1) \equiv 0 \pmod{N}$, so (unless we are very unlucky and $a^{r/2} \equiv \pm 1 \pmod{N}$) $\gcd(a^{r/2} \pm 1, N)$ will give us factors of N. The usual solution to r being odd is to go back and start the classical pre-processing with a different a.

Complexity

Standard complexity theory tells us that the complexity of the classical phases (even if done naïvely) is $O(N^3)$. The quantum phase requires $3n$ qubits (various improvements can apparently cut this down to $2n$). The n vector×matrix multiplications by powers of U_a in Figure 4.3 will take n^2 steps each, i.e. $O(n^3)$. The quantum Fourier transform is $O(n^2)$. Hence, the whole process is $O(n^3)$ operations on $O(n)$ qubits.

This is to be contrasted with the best-known classical algorithm for factoring numbers, the general number field sieve (GNFS; Lenstra et al., 1993a). The running time is generally cited as

$$\exp\left\{\left(\left(\frac{64}{9}\right)^{1/3} + o(1)\right) \log^{1/3} N(\log \log N)^{2/3}\right\} = e^{Cn^{1/3} \log^{2/3} n},$$

where $C = (64/9)^{1/3}/ \log 2 + o(1)$. If N has a special form, e.g. $N = 2^{2^9+1}$ (Lenstra et al., 1993b), the constant C can be rather smaller.

Other Shor uses

Equation (4.5) shows that, given a and N, we can compute r such that $a^r \equiv 1 \pmod{N}$.

The discrete logarithm problem (DLP) is: given g, l and N, find the e such that $g^e \equiv l \pmod{N}$. This is very similar to (4.5), and is basically solved the same way. Breaking DLP breaks Diffie–Hellman key establishment.

The elliptic curve discrete logarithm problem (ECDLP) is the analogy of DLP for elliptic curves. This is very similar to (4.5), and is basically solved the same way. Breaking DLP breaks elliptic curve Diffie–Hellman key establishment and the elliptic curve digital signature algorithm (ECDSA).

QUANTUM KEY DISTRIBUTION

If two participants (call them A and B) have a shared secret, they can use it to derive a key for any one of a variety of encryption methods, for example the Advanced Encryption Standard (AES; Daemen and Rijmen, 2020). But how do they arrange such a shared secret? In the pre-computer age, this was achieved by special messengers carrying code books. But this relied on pre-planning, and wouldn't scale to today's internet, where people wish to purchase from, or contribute to, new sites with which they have no pre-arranged secrets.

This problem was solved by Diffie and Hellman (1976), who used the difficulty of solving a mathematical problem (the **discrete logarithm problem**) as a basis for an ingenious method whereby each participant sent the other a message, and a shared secret was constructed. These days, a slight variant (elliptic curve Diffie–Hellman) is used, but the principle is the same. Alas, Shor's algorithm on a suitably large quantum computer can break these methods. This, and the conventional cryptographic response, is described in Chapter 6.

The quantum alternative

An alternative is to use the basics of quantum mechanics to arrange a secret (via the measurement of certain quanta) openly, but making sure that no one has intercepted those particular quanta. This is known as **quantum key distribution** (QKD), which is rather a misnomer as no key is being distributed. A more appropriate name would be quantum key establishment, as the processes of quantum mechanics are being used to establish a secret key known only to the two participants. In classical key distribution, the same key can be distributed to multiple people (e.g. agents in a cell), whereas the authors know of no QKD method that works for more than two parties.

There are a variety of QKD methods, of which we shall describe a couple, but all known methods have two characteristics that make them less attractive than might appear:

- Since we are relying on quantum mechanics, A and B must actually be able to share quanta. So if A and B are using a fibre optic cable to communicate the quanta, that cable must directly connect A and B, with no repeaters etc. in the way.

- All known schemes rely on A and B sharing an **authenticated** classical communications channel, i.e. A must be sure that the messages come from B, and vice versa. Note that the messages sent on this channel need **not** be secret.

Note that although the second is a substantial problem, it is not quite the show-stopper it might appear. Once the authenticated channel is set up, we can use QKD to create a new secret, then use that secret going forward. Hence, an authentication method with a limited time span (e.g. a signature scheme that could be cracked in a month) would suffice to get the process started.

The Bennett–Brassard scheme

This was the first QKD scheme, introduced by Bennett and Brassard (1984),[5] and is conceptually one of the simplest schemes. It relies on the existence of two conjugate bases, i.e. bases such that measurement in one base is uncorrelated with measurement in the other. While there are several choices for these, we will use the following two, known as ↑ and ↗. Note that, in each basis, one basis vector corresponds to the binary value 0, and the other to 1.

In ↑, the two basis vectors can be thought of as

$$\begin{pmatrix}1\\0\end{pmatrix} \text{ and } \begin{pmatrix}0\\1\end{pmatrix}.$$

In ↗, the two basis vectors can be thought of as

$$\frac{1}{\sqrt{2}}\begin{pmatrix}1\\1\end{pmatrix} \text{ and } \frac{1}{\sqrt{2}}\begin{pmatrix}1\\-1\end{pmatrix}.$$

The process goes through the following four stages.

---

6 While this chapter was being written, it was announced (acm.org/media-center/2026/march/turing-award-2025) that the authors had received the A. M. Turing Award 'for foundational contributions to quantum information science'.

Quantum transmission

A picks a random bit, and a random choice of basis, and sends a single photon representing that bit in that basis to B. A records the choice of bit, choice of basis and time for this transmission. This is repeated until enough bits have been sent. Quantum mechanics means that if an eavesdropper chooses the same basis as A, the eavesdropper will get the same value, but if the other basis is chosen by the eavesdropper, the eavesdropper will get either basis vector (in the eavesdropper's basis) at random **and** the quantum value will be what was measured.

Quantum reception

B measures each photon, using a random basis each time. B records the choice of bit, choice of basis and time for each recording.

Reconciliation

A and B broadcast (on the authenticated channel) the bases they have used, and discard the bits where A and B used different bases (so randomly we have half the bits left). At this point, at least in a perfect world, A and B have a shared bit pattern if there was no interception.

Eavesdropper check

A and B now compare (over the authenticated, but publicly readable channel) a predetermined subset of the bits. If B's measurement differs from A's transmission, then either there has been an actual error, or the eavesdropper has measured (and altered) the bits. If more than p bits differ, A and B give up on this run and start again, possibly using a different quantum channel as this one is probably being intercepted. If not, A and B believe that the shared bit string is largely unintercepted, and use a technique known as **privacy amplification** to reduce the eavesdropper's knowledge further.

The Ekert scheme

This was introduced by Ekert (1991), and is based on entangled photons: someone (A, B or an outsider) gives each of A and

B one photon from an entangled pair. This has the following properties:

- If A and B use the same basis when measuring their photons, they will get the same results.
- No one (A, B or the photon pair generator) can predict the result.
- Any attempt to eavesdrop will destroy this synchronisation.

The basis ↗ we introduced earlier is the 'obvious' basis ↑ rotated by $\pi/4 = 45°$. For this method, we also need →, which is the obvious basis rotated by $\pi/2$, and ↘, which is the obvious basis rotated by $3\pi/4$.

A's quantum reception

A measures A's photon from each pair, randomly using ↑, ↗ or →. A records the basis, result and time.

B's quantum reception

B measures B's photon from each pair, randomly using ↗, → or ↘. B records the basis, result and time.

Reconciliation

A and B broadcast (on the authenticated channel) the bases they have used, and separate the bit positions into two groups: those where they used the same bases, and those where they have used different bases.

Eavesdropper check

For the second group, they share values (which may well be different, of course) and compute a test statistic S to check that these have the behaviour that would be expected. The perfect value of S is $\pm 2\sqrt{2}$. Should $|S|$ be significantly less than $2\sqrt{2}$ (where 'significantly' depends on the error rate of the process), then eavesdropping is suspected. Otherwise the bits in the first group can be used as a shared secret.

QKD in practice

There are many other variants of quantum key distribution, but the core idea that we cannot prevent, but can detect, eavesdropping is the same. Also, all of them require an authenticated classical channel, i.e. one that the eavesdropper can read but cannot tamper with (without being detected). Numerous uses of QKD are given in Aquina et al. (2025, §4).

One well-documented example is given by Yin et al. (2020), which describes 'entanglement-based QKD between two ground stations separated by 1,120 kilometres at a finite secret-key rate of 0.12 bits per second, without the need for trusted relays. Entangled photon pairs were distributed via two bidirectional downlinks from the Micius satellite to two ground observatories in Delingha and Nanshan in China' (p. 501). Although this used entanglement (as a means of not needing to trust the satellite), it used Bennett et al. (1992) rather than Ekert (1991) as the detailed mechanism.

Relays

The first problem we mentioned for practical QKD is that A and B need to able to share quanta. Suppose they can't, but both can share quanta with a trusted intermediary I, who can act as a relay. Then A can think of a classical secret *s*, and engage in QKD with I to convey *s* to I. I can decrypt this, then engage in QKD with B to transfer *s* to B. A and B then share a key *s*, which is secure as long as they trust I not to remember *s* and not to transfer it to anyone else.

But suppose they don't totally trust I, but conversely there are several possible relays I_i who can share quanta with A and with B. Then A can think of multiple secrets s_i, and convey each s_i to B via I_i. Then the actual key that A and B use is the exclusive or of the s_i. This is secret unless all the I_i are not just individually dishonest but actually collude to share the s_i. There is more analysis of this in Robertson et al. (2026).

Quantum key distribution or post-quantum cryptography

So should we move from today's quantum-vulnerable Diffie–Hellman (basic or elliptic curve) to the post-quantum schemes outlined in Chapter 6, or to the QKD techniques outlined in this chapter? There is a significant comparison of QKD and PQC in Aquina et al. (2025).

Multi-party quantum key agreement

In the previous sections we have explained how A and B can agree a key. In the methods we have described (and all others the authors know of) both parties contribute to the key. No external eavesdropper can observe the key **undetected**, and this is essentially the only threat considered.

As pointed out in Mouaji and Al-Kuwari (2026), once we ask for genuine multi-party key agreement there are issues of internal fairness, ensuring that no subset of dishonest participants can precompute or manipulate the agreed-upon key, as well as external eavesdropper detection.

5 ARCHITECTURAL MODELS

Stefano Mensa, Michael Garn and David Galvin

INTRODUCTION

'Not all qubits were created equal.' This common statement in the quantum computing community captures the diverse, complex and rapidly evolving nature of quantum computing's current technology landscape. While qubits serve the same fundamental purpose of storing and processing quantum information, they do so in very different ways, depending on the physical system used to create and manipulate them. A qubit can be represented in several ways, for example by a photon, a neutral atom or a trapped ion; each comes with an individual set of strengths, weaknesses and technological challenges due to its particular physical nature. At the time of writing, there is no clear indication about which technology is going to deliver **useful** quantum computing, and the race towards the creation of scalable, high-quality and reliable qubits is on. Understanding the differences between qubits is key to appreciating the diverse approaches to building quantum computers and how this directly shapes the future of the field and its applications. This chapter provides an overview of the major types of quantum computing devices, each based on a different physical implementation of qubits: superconducting qubits, photonics, trapped ions and neutral atoms. This is then contextualised with the state of today's quantum devices, also known as NISQ devices (see Chapter 1), followed by a discussion on the future of quantum computing, fault-tolerant quantum computing.

QUBIT TECHNOLOGIES

Quantum computing with superconductors

There is great interest in using superconducting technology to create quantum computing devices; it has become the basis of quantum technology from a wide variety of technology providers, from blue-chip companies such as Google and IBM to more recently founded businesses such as Rigetti, IQM and D-Wave. **Superconductivity** is a peculiar property of certain materials where the electrical resistance in the material drops to zero at exceptionally low temperatures, allowing a free flow of electrical current. In practice, to make a quantum computing device this phenomenon can be leveraged with a device known as a Josephson junction. This is created by using insulating material placed between two superconducting materials in a circuit, and allows nonlinear quantum tunnelling effects to carry superconducting current across a thin insulated barrier. This can help in the construction of what is often described as an 'artificial atom'.

This concept, in this context, is fundamental to creating and controlling quantum information. In this setup, certain parts of the circuit can hold paired electrons at specific energy levels that can represent quantum states – the qubits. Microwave pulses can then be used to control and read these states, hence controlling and producing information. However, superconducting properties are only possible if the device is cooled to very low temperatures (fraction of a kelvin), and the device must be cooled at all times in order to maintain superconductivity and not lose the information being created and manipulated.

Superconducting hardware is an inviting prospect for quantum computing and a variety of architectures with different qubit layouts have been developed to realise the universal gate-based model of quantum computation that is fundamental for general quantum computing applications. Constructing multi-qubit gates by coupling circuits via an intermediate circuit element naturally introduces design complexity when considering many spatially separated qubits, leading to a large number of (potentially noisy) swap operations to allow interactions, and exchange of information, between distant qubits. Indeed, algorithms that rely on the use of multi-qubit couplings carry the additional design consideration of how these qubits can be related through the network topology of the device: qubit connectivity. The efficient routing of interactions between qubits in an algorithm is itself a complex problem, and heuristics are needed to break down the steps of the algorithm into gates and routing (swaps). Performing this process (**transpilation**) in a way that allows the algorithm to still be performant highlights a key consideration for mapping and deploying algorithms on superconducting architectures, namely how the algorithm is affected by the relative positioning of the qubits encoding the problem and the quality of the connecting edges.

The interested reader can find more accessible information about superconducting quantum computing in the review in Kjaergaard et al. (2020).

Quantum computing with trapped ions

The use of trapped ions (TIs) as qubits is one of the earliest viable implementations of quantum computers, conceptualised in the 1990s and demonstrated in practice in the early 2000s. TIs as building blocks for quantum computers have been a subject of research for nearly 30 years, with groups at Oxford, Cambridge, Southampton and Sussex universities and Imperial College leading the way in the UK. A few notable UK-based university spinouts using TI technology to deliver quantum computers include Oxford Ionics and Universal Quantum. In the US, companies such as IonQ and Quantinuum have been at the forefront of developing trapped ion quantum computers, delivering commercially available machines for industry use either on-premises or via the cloud.

The relevance of TI quantum computers comes from the fact that the so-called DiVincenzo criteria – the five basic requirements for universal quantum computing (DiVincenzo,

2000) – have all been demonstrated using systems with a few trapped ions. Specifically, the criteria are: (1) the capability of having well-defined two-level qubits; (2) the ability to initialise a qubit to a well-defined state; (3) the qubit decoherence time is longer than the quantum gate time; (4) qubits can be manipulated with a set of universal quantum gates; (5) high-accuracy qubit readout.

TI quantum computers use ions (charged atoms) held in place (trapped) by electromagnetic fields as qubits. Atoms of particular elements are suitable for the task, chosen thanks to their capability of ionising (becoming charged atoms) when excited using a light source (a laser) tuned to a specific wavelength and able to provide enough energy to the atom to excite one electron from a relaxed, ground-state energy to an excited state. Applied to qubits, the ground state represents $|0\rangle$, the excited state $|1\rangle$. To fully manipulate ions and perform computation, their motion must be constrained both in terms of spatial position and speed, via **trapping** (using radio frequencies) and laser cooling. Using these two approaches, it is possible to use single-qubit gates and two-qubit (entangling) gates. Interested readers wanting to know more about this technology can refer to the review in Bernardini (2024).

The physical properties of TI systems provide some significant advantages over other common quantum computing technologies. First, coherence times are often remarkably long, meaning that the TI can hold on to its quantum state for a significant amount of time before it is disrupted by external noise, which helps provide reliable computation. Second, gate operations (both single- and two-qubit) have very high fidelities, resulting in better-quality gate operations and accurate results.

However, the technology also has several downsides that currently limit the scalability of the method. One practical drawback of the implementation of TI systems is that the absolute gate speed is significantly lower (ca. 10^{-6} s) than other qubit technologies such as superconducting qubits (ca. 10^{-9} s), with variations between TI vendors and prototypes.

This has a direct implication on the speed of algorithmic execution, predicted to be much slower for some common algorithms such as factorisation. Finally, trapping large numbers of ions simultaneously and controlling them is a major technological obstacle to the scalability of such devices, a particular challenge being implementing the necessary control components.

Quantum computing with photons

Research into scalable photonic quantum computing began in the 1990s (Cerf et al., 1998), with significant progress marked by the introduction in the 2000s of the KLM scheme (Knill et al., 2001), showing that quantum computation could be efficiently simulated using linear optics. Linear optical quantum computing (LOQC) is notable for its potential scalability and its ability to leverage existing optical technologies, though challenges to large-scale implementation include photon loss, the development of on-demand single-photon sources and limited photon detector efficiency (O'Brien, 2007). Notable companies advancing photonic quantum computing with different approaches include Orca Computing, PsiQuantum, Quandela and Xanadu.

To summarise briefly, an LOQC system uses photons or entangled pairs generated by lasers, with quantum information encoded in properties such as polarisation or path, typically in binary states (0 or 1). These photons then pass through linear optical circuits containing elements like beam splitters and phase shifters, where superposition and interference enable quantum logic operations. Finally, quantum information is extracted by measuring the properties in question. For a thorough review, see, for example, Kok et al. (2007). Note that LOQC is inherently probabilistic due to the difficulty of deterministically generating entanglement and executing entangling gates. However, measurement-based quantum computing (MBQC) provides a natural framework for LOQC (Nielsen, 2006; Raussendorf and Briegel, 2001), as information is processed by first preparing an initial multiparty entangled state offline. Once the resource is prepared correctly, computation is carried out by performing measurements in a specific pattern. These measurements induce nonunitary operations, which can nevertheless simulate gates within the circuit model.

Quantum photonic computers, whether using discrete-variable (DV) or continuous-variable (CV) architectures (Slussarenko and Pryde, 2019; Braunstein and Van Loock, 2005), are still relatively new compared to matter-based approaches, such as superconducting quantum computers, which have made rapid progress in both device size and functionality. While DV systems, which encode information in binary states like polarisation, are closer to established qubit models, both DV and CV photonic systems face unique technical challenges. Key components, such as high-efficiency photon sources, precise detectors and robust quantum gates, are actively being developed. If the fundamental challenges of on-demand single-photon sources and deterministic entanglement can be overcome, LOQC platforms have a high potential for miniaturisation and scalability.

Quantum computing with neutral atoms

Neutral atom architectures use large arrays of atoms trapped in an optical lattice, encoding the qubit states within the energy levels of the trapped atoms, with control, addressing and basic gate operations performed via laser pulse or 'optical tweezers'. Proponents of this approach have pointed to the naturally long coherence times associated with such electronic encoded qubits, which may use 'hyperfine' ground states generated by nuclear–electronic interactions in single atoms. A major challenge for this approach is two-qubit gate operations (Jaksch et al., 2000), which require entanglement generation between paired atoms in the lattice without the introduction of decoherence.

Typical proposals for multi-qubit gates involve the use of Rydberg atoms, which are atoms whose valence electrons have been excited to a very high energy state, and some have made use of the so-called 'Rydberg blockade', an effect in which double excitation between neighbouring Rydberg atoms is energetically forbidden (Browaeys et al., 2016). With research ongoing, proponents of the architecture believe that neutral atom arrays with coherent shuttling of information represent a major candidate for scalable quantum computations (Bluvstein et al., 2022). At the time of writing, companies such as QuEra and Infleqtion have developed roadmaps using neutral atom technology.

Qubits using neutral atoms carry a benefit compared to solid-state designs owing to the lack of potential for manufacturing defects in the physical qubit itself, ensuring better fidelity and uniformity in quality. Moreover, the scalability that comes with neutral atom designs provides strong potential for error correction, which can carry a high resource cost in physical qubits; however, this must be qualified by identifying the associated costs in scaling the laser-optical set up and the hard-to-correct errors associated with Rydberg states. Neutral atom technology can in principle operate at 'room temperature', with atomic cooling being achieved through the high degree of local control offered by the lasers. Although neutral atom architectures boast 'all-to-all' connectivity in principle, the physical requirements for moving atomic qubits in this approach leads to a trade-off in longer times for gate operations.

A more robust summary of neutral atom quantum computing can be found in Wintersperger et al. (2023).

THE CURRENT STATE: THE NISQ ERA

Questions that are often asked of quantum computing technologists and scientists are, what are quantum computers useful for? And what can we do with them **today**? The answer to both questions is uncertain and polarised, depending on who is answering – quantum computing providers, scientists or end users. However, there is one key challenge that everyone agrees on, regardless of their viewpoint: noise is a major obstacle that continues to hinder the full potential of this emerging technology.

Noisy intermediate-scale quantum (NISQ) devices broadly refers to devices with qubit counts in the region of fifty to hundreds. The adjective 'noisy' means that the qubits used to perform computations via a series of single and entangling gates are subject to interference coming from different sources – thermal fluctuation, mechanical vibration, decoherence and so forth – which ultimately has an impact on the quality of the output of the computation and depends on the quantum technology used. Simply, the result that we extrapolate is not ideal and deviates from the desired outcome, which eventually has an impact on the reliability of the available quantum computers. The type of noise is mostly dependent on the technology used to design the quantum device; however, currently no technology is free from it.

Noise has major implications on the applicability of quantum computers in every domain area. Take, for example, the famous quantum approximate optimisation algorithm (QAOA), which is designed to help solve combinatorial optimisation problems like finding the shortest path through a network or the best arrangement of items. The output of such an algorithm is a series of strings of bits, or answers to the problem, which are then used to explore different solutions to the problem. In an ideal, noiseless, scenario, the algorithm would produce high-quality solutions to the problem. In practice, NISQ devices will produce an array of solutions that is in fact sub-optimal, where the bit-strings are corrupted and hence suggest sub-optimal solutions to the problem, often making it impossible to distinguish the right answer from the wrong ones.

To make quantum devices useful and unlock the transformative potential that this technology promises to bring at scale, the community must first deal with noise, identifying strategies to mitigate and eventually correct its effects on computations. All the major qubit technologies are increasing the available number of qubits for computations, making it possible to perform calculations of increasingly complex problems, while also introducing new algorithmic solutions towards error mitigation. To date, users can perform calculations on hundreds of qubits and see tangible differences in the quality and utility of the devices as new error mitigation strategies emerge. However, to achieve the full quantum advantage the journey towards scalability and full error correction has yet to be finished.

THE FUTURE VISION: FAULT-TOLERANT QUANTUM COMPUTING

The achievement of scalable, useful and general quantum computing will only be possible with the advent of fault-tolerant quantum computing (FTQC). This term indicates a generic category of devices that are capable of performing quantum computations at scale and being able to use error correction techniques to withstand the errors that arise during the process. Algorithms that require many qubits and use very deep gate circuits (e.g. Shor's algorithm) are designed to function on such devices, and their implementation currently lies sometime in the future.

Reflecting on the current state of quantum computing and its direction opens further questions and considerations with respect to its adoption – should industry adopt the technology experimentally now, using NISQ devices, or should it wait for the first true FTQC systems and prepare itself for their arrival at scale? There is no right or wrong answer, and both avenues come with pros and cons. Accepting that NISQ devices are limited in size and application reach, their usage would enable industry to get comfortable with the technology and start prototyping applications, uses and integration while upskilling its workforce. Some businesses recognise that quantum computing **will** solve critical challenges, but in the FTQC future, and it becomes more valuable to design algorithms that will solve the challenge when the first FTQC devices are available.

Regardless of the adoption direction chosen and the quantum technology used, the future of quantum computing is fault tolerant. Each quantum computing technology offers unique strengths and faces distinct challenges. Superconductors, trapped ions, photons, topological qubits and neutral atoms represent just a few of the many avenues researchers are exploring to realise the potential of quantum computing. As the field advances, we may see one or more of these approaches emerge as the dominant technology, or perhaps a hybrid approach will lead the way ahead of FTQC.

6 POST-QUANTUM CRYPTOGRAPHY

James Davenport and Jeremy Green

INTRODUCTION

Imagine sending a letter today that you need to remain secret for the next 30 years. You lock it in the strongest safe you can find, confident in its protection. But what if, 25 years from now, someone invents a device that can see through thick steel to reveal the contents? Your secret would be exposed, not because the safe was flawed, but because the assumptions underpinning its security had been rendered obsolete.

This is the challenge we face with quantum computing. The cryptographic algorithms that protect our digital world, from online banking to private messages, all rely on mathematical problems that are hard for today's computers to solve. Quantum computers, however, promise to solve these problems with terrifying ease. Post-quantum cryptography (PQC) is building new cryptographic algorithms that remain secure even when quantum computers arrive, then ensuring these are implemented. However, a lot of encrypted data has already been stolen and sits waiting for the day it can be decrypted – this is called 'harvest now, decrypt later'.

WHAT IS PQC?

Post-quantum cryptography refers to cryptographic algorithms designed to be secure against attack by both classical computers (the ones we use today) and quantum computers. Unlike the systems we currently rely on, PQC does not depend on mathematical problems that quantum algorithms like Shor's can break.

This is not a minor upgrade or a simple patch. PQC represents a complete replacement of the cryptographic foundation upon which modern digital trust is built. Every time you visit a secure website, send an encrypted email or install a software update, you are relying on classical cryptography that will potentially fail; this applies particularly to current asymmetric cryptography.

THE QUANTUM THREAT

To understand why PQC is essential, we must first understand what quantum computers can do to our current systems.

Shor's algorithm

Mathematician Peter Shor developed an algorithm that would change the course of cryptography forever. When run on a sufficiently powerful quantum computer, Shor's algorithm, covered in detail in Chapter 4, can efficiently solve two mathematical problems:

- integer factorisation, by finding the prime numbers that multiply to give a larger number;
- discrete logarithms, by solving for the exponent in certain mathematical equations.

Why does this matter? Because nearly all public-key cryptography used today such as RSA, elliptic curve cryptography (ECC) and Diffie–Hellman key exchange derives its security from the difficulty of exactly these problems.

A large-scale quantum computer running Shor's algorithm could:

- decrypt any message encrypted with RSA;
- forge any digital signature protected by ECC;
- impersonate any user or website whose identity relies on these schemes.

This is not a distant theoretical threat. As discussed in earlier chapters, progress towards cryptographically relevant quantum computers is accelerating, with major vendors projecting capability within the next decade.

Grover's algorithm

Symmetric cryptography, such as the Advanced Encryption Standard (AES), fares better, but is not immune to the threat posed by quantum computing. Grover's algorithm, covered in more detail in Chapter 4, provides a quadratic speedup for searching unsorted databases. In cryptographic terms, this means it effectively halves the security strength of symmetric algorithms.

AES-256, which provides 256 bits of security against classical attacks, would provide only 128 bits of effective security against a quantum adversary using Grover's algorithm. While this remains secure for now (NIST recommends AES-256 as a baseline for PQC migration[1]), it demonstrates that even our strongest symmetric algorithms are not untouched by the quantum threat.

THE FOUR TEMPORAL THREAT MODELS

The urgency surrounding PQC is not solely about the day a quantum computer first breaks RSA. The threat is already here, manifesting in four distinct ways. Understanding these temporal threat models helps explain why waiting to see what happens next is not an option.

Harvest now, decrypt later (HNDL)

This is the most widely recognised threat. Adversaries such as nation states, cybercriminal syndicates and corporate

---

1 The argument that AES-256 only provides 128 bits of effective security against Grover is debunked in Chapter 4. Nevertheless, NIST recommends the full 256, probably because it's simpler to explain. A similar argument also applies to hash functions, the other building block vulnerable to Grover's algorithm.

espionage units are currently intercepting and storing vast amounts of encrypted communications. They cannot read them now, but they have assumed they will be able to in the future.

Medical records, government intelligence, trade secrets and personal communications are all at risk now. If you have data that must remain confidential for decades, the encryption protecting it may be sufficient today, but it will be worthless once quantum decryption becomes possible.

Harvest now, forge later (HNFL)

Encryption is not the only target – digital signatures are equally vulnerable. Adversaries can collect signed artefacts today, for example software updates, firmware images, legal documents and digital certificates, with the intention of forging them later.

This is not a confidentiality threat, it is an integrity threat. Imagine a system where software updates are signed with a quantum-vulnerable algorithm. Years later, an attacker could forge a signature for malicious code, and systems trusting that old, now-broken signature would accept it as genuine. Trusted records could be rewritten, audit trails manipulated and counterfeit certificates created.

Trust now, forge later (TNFL)

This extends HNFL into the very infrastructure of trust. Our entire public-key infrastructure (PKI) – the system of certificates and authorities that authenticates websites, devices and people – relies on digital signatures that will become forgeable.

The trust anchors we rely on today become open to counterfeit tomorrow. An adversary could:

- impersonate any device or service;
- fabricate entire certificate chains;
- subvert firmware update ecosystems;

- manipulate safety-critical systems that depend on signed commands.

TNFL is particularly dangerous for operational technology – systems controlling power grids, water treatment and manufacturing – where signed commands directly affect physical processes.

Deploy now, exploit later (DNEL)

This threat addresses lifecycle exposure. Many devices deployed today will remain in service for decades: industrial controllers, medical implants, electric vehicle charging stations, automotive electronic control units, IoT sensors. If these devices cannot be upgraded to support PQC because they lack processing power, have no update mechanism or are simply forgotten, they become permanently vulnerable.

DNEL is a cyber physical safety threat. An attacker could, years from now, impersonate or compromise devices that cannot rotate their keys, creating persistent footholds in critical infrastructure and enabling attacks on vehicles, energy systems and medical devices. This is the most structurally difficult threat to mitigate because it arises from design choices made years before quantum exploitation will become possible.

NIST PQC STANDARDS

Recognising the urgency of this threat, the US National Institute of Standards and Technology (NIST) launched a multi-year international competition to identify, evaluate and standardise post-quantum cryptographic algorithms. On 13 August 2024, NIST released the first three Federal Information Processing Standards (FIPS) for PQC, as described below.[2]

2 For further reading, see NIST's Post-Quantum Cryptography Project, csrc.nist.gov/projects/post-quantum-cryptography; FIPS 203 (ML-KEM), Module-Lattice-Based Key-Encapsulation Mechanism Standard; FIPS 204 (ML-DSA), Module-Lattice-Based Digital Signature Standard; FIPS 205 (SLH-DSA), Stateless Hash-Based Digital Signature Standard; NIST IR 8547: Transitioning the Use of Cryptographic Algorithms and Key Lengths.

These three standards are not the end of the story. NIST continues to evaluate additional algorithms, including Falcon (an alternative lattice-based signature scheme) and HQC (a code-based key encapsulation mechanism), to serve as backups or to address specific use cases.

FIPS 203: ML-KEM

Derived from the CRYSTALS-Kyber algorithm, this is the primary standard for encryption and key establishment. ML-KEM (module lattice-based key encapsulation mechanism) is designed to replace RSA and Diffie–Hellman/elliptic curve Diffie–Hellman for key exchange in protocols like TLS (the technology behind HTTPS). However, RSA signatures are replaced with ML DSA and SLH DSA. It provides a secure way for two parties to agree on a shared secret key without an eavesdropper being able to determine it even with a quantum computer.

FIPS 204: ML-DSA

Based on CRYSTALS-Dilithium, this standard provides a high-performance digital signature scheme. Digital signatures are used everywhere: to verify software updates, sign documents, authenticate users and secure blockchain transactions. ML-DSA (module lattice-based digital signature algorithm) is designed to be the workhorse for general-purpose digital signatures in the quantum era.

FIPS 205: SLH-DSA

Derived from SPHINCS+, this scheme offers a more conservative approach to digital signature. Instead of relying on lattice-based mathematics, SLH-DSA (stateless hash-based digital signature algorithm) bases its security entirely on the properties of cryptographic hash functions, a well-understood and trusted foundation.

SPECIFIC USE CASES

It is often said that a major problem with post-quantum cryptography is that key sizes get bigger. This is true, but the details are subtler, and depend on the method chosen, as shown in Table 6.1 (Buchanan, 2024). As we can see, Crystals and SLH-DSA are incomparable. For the commonest application (TLS certificates) we want a signed public key, so we see that Crystals Dilithium (ML-DSA) is significantly better than SLH-DSA. But different applications may well have different views.

Table 6.1 Comparison of encryption algorithms

Name	Public key size	Private key size	Signature size	Security level
RSA-2048	256	256	256	1
ECDSA	64	32	32	1
Crystals Dilithium 2	1,312	2,528	2,420	1
Crystals Dilithium 3	1,952	4,000	3,293	3
Crystals Dilithium 5	2,592	4,864	4,595	5
SLH-DSA-SHA2-128f	32	64	17,088	1
SLH-DSA-SHA2-192f	48	96	35,664	3
SLH-DSA-SHA2-256f	64	128	49,856	5

THE MIGRATION CHALLENGE

If PQC standards exist, why not simply switch everything over tomorrow? The answer lies in the enormous scale and complexity of the task.

Cryptographic agility

The ideal state, cryptographic agility, is the ability to rapidly replace or upgrade cryptographic algorithms without major system redesign. A crypto agile system can negotiate which algorithm to use, support multiple algorithms simultaneously during transition and seamlessly adopt new standards as they emerge.

Most existing systems are not crypto agile. Cryptography is often hard coded, deeply embedded and tightly coupled with application logic. Achieving agility requires:

- abstracting cryptographic operations behind flexible APIs;
- designing protocols that support algorithm negotiation;
- building inventory systems that track where every cryptographic asset is used;
- establishing governance processes to manage the lifecycle of algorithms.

Long lead time

Infrastructure changes slowly. Consider the following lifespans:

- web servers and applications: 3–5 years;
- network equipment: 5–8 years;
- industrial control systems: 10–20 years, or longer in the case of building controls;
- embedded devices in cars or medical equipment: 15–30 years.

Systems being designed and deployed today will still be operational when quantum computers capable of breaking RSA arrive. If they cannot be upgraded to PQC, they become permanent vulnerabilities. This is why migration planning must begin now, even for systems that will not be fully replaced for years.

When the industry transitioned from SHA-1 to SHA-2 (a much simpler cryptographic upgrade), the process took approximately 12 years from standardisation to widespread completion. Organisations faced incompatibilities, legacy integrations and staffing shortages. Nearly two decades later, some systems still rely on SHA-1.

The PQC transition is orders of magnitude more complex. It involves replacing the foundational public-key infrastructure that underpins all digital trust. Every certificate, every protocol, every embedded device must be assessed, updated or replaced.

Legacy systems and operational technology

The hardest challenge is not modern servers and applications, it is the vast ecosystem of legacy and operational technology. These systems:

- often run on limited hardware incapable of PQC's computational demands;
- may have no update mechanism or vendor support;
- are frequently critical to safety or operations;
- can be prohibitively expensive to replace.

For these systems, direct PQC migration may be impossible. Compensating controls such as network segmentation, intrusion detection and physical security become essential. Organisations must accept that some systems will remain vulnerable and manage that risk through other means.

Cost and resources

PQC migration is not free. It requires:

- investment in inventory and discovery tools;
- staff training and expertise development;
- testing and validation in staging environments;
- vendor engagement and supply chain assessment;
- potential hardware upgrades or replacements;
- ongoing monitoring and governance.

For resource-constrained organisations like small businesses, local government and educational institutions, these costs are significant. Yet the cost of a future breach, especially for long-lived sensitive data, is far higher.

- Medical records must remain confidential for a patient's lifetime.
- Government classified information may need protection for decades.
- Financial transactions and audit logs must be trustworthy for regulatory periods.
- Personal communications and photos may be sensitive for generations.

Any organisation holding such data, and that includes most of us, whether as individuals or institutions, needs to plan for PQC migration. The threat is not 'if' but 'when', and the attackers are already collecting.

Standards will evolve

NIST's work continues. New algorithms will be added, and if vulnerabilities are discovered in the current ones, replacements will be needed. The cryptographic landscape will remain dynamic for the foreseeable future.

CONCLUSION

Post-quantum cryptography is the single most important initiative in cybersecurity today. It is the only known defence against a threat that will eventually render our current cryptographic infrastructure obsolete. The release of NIST's first PQC standards in August 2024 marked the beginning of a new era, one in which we must systematically replace the algorithms that have protected us for decades but, as we head towards quantum supremacy, are now vulnerable.

The challenge is immense, involving inventorying cryptographic assets, achieving crypto agility, managing legacy systems, training staff and navigating a multi-year migration – but the cost of inaction is greater. The adversaries are already harvesting data, already collecting signed artefacts, positioning themselves for the day when quantum computers can break insecure cryptographic protocols.

PQC is not a supplement to existing security. It is a replacement. It is not a one-time project either but an ongoing commitment. For anyone responsible for protecting sensitive data, whether a CISO, a system administrator or an individual, planning must start now.

Here is a high-level practical roadmap to support PQC migration and quantum computing.

Inventory everything

You cannot protect what you do not know you have. Create a complete registry of:

- cryptographic algorithms and key lengths;
- certificates and their expiration dates;
- protocols (TLS, SSH, IPsec, VPNs);
- libraries and their versions;
- devices and embedded systems;
- third-party dependencies.

Classify by risk

Not all data needs the same protection. Identify:

- data requiring long-term confidentiality (10+ years);
- systems that cannot be easily upgraded;
- critical infrastructure and safety-related controls;
- high-value targets for adversaries.

Build crypto agility

Design new systems to support algorithm negotiation and easy replacement. For existing systems, plan upgrades that introduce abstraction layers where possible. The goal is to make cryptographic transitions routine rather than revolutionary.

Engage your supply chain

Your security depends on your vendors. Ask:

- What is their PQC roadmap?
- Do their products support crypto agility?
- Can they provide evidence of quantum readiness?

Include PQC requirements in contracts and procurement.

Train your people

Educate everyone, from the boardroom to the server room. Executives need to understand the business risk; engineers need to know how to implement PQC safely; users need to recognise that the threat is real and action is required.

Start piloting

You do not need to migrate everything at once. Begin with:

- hybrid TLS experiments using PQC key exchange;

- PQC-enabled certificates for test systems;
- vendor pilots for new products.

Learn what works in your environment before scaling.

HYBRID KEY EXCHANGE

We may well be reluctant to abandon tried-and-trusted methods of key establishment, with decades of use against all known classical attacks, for these new-fangled quantum schemes whose advantages are currently hypothetical. Hence TLS implementations are moving to hybrid schemes, which use both classical and post-quantum techniques that are secure if either is broken. Table 6.2 (Fall, 2025) shows some current implementations.

Table 6.2 Hybrid key exchange schemes

Hybrid scheme	Organisation	Implementation	Forward security	Reference
Kyber–ECDH	Cloudflare and Google	Kyber/X25519	Yes (X25519)	Bindel et al. (2019)
Kyber–ECDH	OpenSSH	Kyber/ECDH	Yes (ECDH)	Hülsing et al. (2021)
Kyber–ECDH	Google and Cisco	IPSec + Kyber/DH or ECDH	Yes with IKEv2	Sikeridis et al. (2020)
Kyber–RSA or ECDH	IETF			Reddy and Tschofenig (2025)

Connolly et al. (2026b) recently produced a proof that a particular combination scheme (Connolly et al., 2026a) is safe if either the classical scheme or the post-quantum scheme is broken.

Monitor and adapt

The quantum landscape will continue to evolve. New algorithms will be standardised; new attacks may be discovered. Establish processes to track developments and update your plans accordingly.

7 WIDER IMPLICATIONS

Jamie Kavanagh

INTRODUCTION

> 'Quantum computing is just five years away from completely transforming the world'
>
> – Overheard by me at the bar of a BCS event. It was late into the evening... June 2023

Quantum computing is indeed approaching the threshold of application in the real world, bringing with it the promise of a new quantum age, and all sorts of unprecedented discoveries. With its much-touted ability to solve complex problems in mere nanoseconds, what does this mean for the world at large? What does it mean for us?

Like many great technological advancements, people are naturally rather blinkered in their hopes for a panacea that will solve the world's woes and usher in an age of hope and wonder. I remember first hearing about ChatGPT, and my innate love of science fiction fuelled endless daydreams of solving global crises, answering the philosophical and metaphysical conundrums of humanity and its place in the universe, and of having someone else check and respond to my hundreds of emails a day. All truly noble causes. However, that dream was firmly shattered after my first attempt at asking it to rubber duck some code I was writing. I shan't be duped again!

So, we must not be distracted by promises without first understanding the terms. It's a tough task, and not always possible, to pre-empt the ways in which the world will use new inventions. Even noble intentions can make us blind to catastrophic consequences. Don't forget, the plastic bag was invented to stop the cutting of trees to make paper bags. Look how that turned out.

As something of a quantum outsider, instead of qubits and entanglement, I want to introduce you to the wider implications of quantum computing. Where I have no talent for physics, what I can offer expertise on is inclusive governance, the ethical use of technology, and community and societal cohesion. In this chapter I'm going to explore a limited selection of ethical and societal flashpoints in quantum computing. My aim here isn't to provide a complete treatise on the ethics of quantum computing, nor an exhaustive list of contingency or risk aversion strategies for the implementation and use of this technology. My aim is to simply start with the interesting question of what might happen if quantum computing is left to develop unchecked, and then explore the real-world ethical, regulatory, societal and global impacts and opportunities of that question.

ETHICAL AND REGULATORY CONSIDERATIONS

Quantum computing's power is highly likely to magnify some familiar technological ethics issues, while simultaneously introducing completely new ones.

Privacy and security

One of the foremost concerns arising from quantum computing is in privacy and security. When a sufficiently advanced quantum computer is developed, it may eventually break the advanced encryption algorithms that currently safeguard much of our digital data.

In practice, this means encrypted communications, financial transactions and government secrets considered highly secure today could be decrypted in the future if attackers gain access to quantum technologies.

The National Institute of Standards and Technology (NIST) have theorised that 'a quantum computer capable of breaking 2000-bit RSA [the Rivest–Shamir–Adleman cryptosystem] in a matter of hours could be built by 2030 for a budget of about a billion dollars' (Chen et al., 2016).

This threat is not a hollow one. Security experts are already warning about 'harvest now, decrypt later' (HNDL) attacks, where malicious entities harvest encrypted data today in order to decrypt it once quantum tools become available (see Chapter 6). Imagine national secrets, financial and personal information, and proprietary organisational property being held for ransom, or worse yet used to undermine public trust, sow discontent and damage economic markets, by bad actors – an unsettling thought.

Algorithmic fairness

Algorithmic fairness is another pressing concern of quantum computing. If quantum computing is applied in areas like artificial intelligence or big data analytics, there is a risk that it could inadvertently introduce bias, or even worsen bias we are already detecting, in automated decisions.

Quantum algorithms trained on biased datasets might produce skewed or discriminatory outcomes, just as classical algorithms can. In fact, some experts suggest that quantum computing's complexity could magnify existing algorithmic bias issues, making them even harder to detect and explain (Kahana, 2020). A quantum-accelerated AI system with unresolved bias has the potential to make inequitable decisions at an alarming rate. Think of the potential impact that might have on recruitment, or financial lending.

This has led to calls for mitigating controls such as rigorous bias testing or licensing requirements for sensitive quantum AI applications, to prevent negative outcomes (Kahana, 2020). The driving principle here is that greater computing power doesn't immediately mean better results, and it certainly doesn't exempt us from the accountability standards we apply to technology. If anything, it heightens the need for oversight to ensure quantum-powered systems treat individuals and groups fairly.

Equal access

A broader ethical imperative is equitable access to the benefits of quantum technology. This is a wicked issue, for it exists in a world of competing agendas, perceptions and appetite for change.

Because quantum computing research requires substantial resources, its advantages might initially be confined to well-funded governments and corporations. This raises the question of whether the rise of quantum computing will create a new 'quantum divide' between the few who can leverage the technology and the many who cannot (Hidary and Sarkar, 2023). As of early 2023, only 17 countries had invested in a national quantum R&D programme, while more than 150 countries had none (Hidary and Sarkar, 2023). If left unaddressed, disparities in access to quantum could exacerbate global inequality and leave many communities unable to benefit from (or defend against) quantum breakthroughs (Hidary and Sarkar, 2023).

It's hard to pinpoint exactly what impacts might look like due to the unique requirements, social barriers and make-up of communities – particularly those that are marginalised or isolated. What we can infer is a widening socio-economic and educational divide between communities who are and are not able to utilise advanced technologies.

Ethically, there is an imperative to broaden participation in quantum computing. This means promoting inclusivity in quantum education and research globally, to ensure that developing nations, smaller companies and underrepresented groups can share in the technology's gains and have a voice in how it's used (Hidary and Sarkar, 2023). The World Economic Forum's Quantum Computing Governance project, for example, emphasises that ethical concerns are only just beginning to be discussed and that global guidelines do not yet exist, highlighting the need for collaborative efforts to set principles for responsible quantum development (Coates et al., 2022).

How are policymakers and institutions responding to these challenges?

The regulatory and governance landscape for quantum computing is still in its infancy. Unlike mature domains like medicine, aviation, finance etc., we don't yet have specific laws or treaties for quantum technology. However, groundwork is being laid. International bodies and industry groups have started crafting technical standards and ethical frameworks.

Standards

The Institute of Electrical and Electronics Engineers (IEEE) and International Organization for Standardization (ISO) have working groups on quantum computing standards, aiming to ensure safety and interoperability as the technology evolves.

The World Economic Forum and other multi-stakeholder groups are actively discussing quantum ethics and governance principles, drawing on lessons from AI ethics and cybersecurity to propose guidelines before quantum computers become widespread (Coates et al., 2022). The thinking is that the best time to address ethical implications is during the design phase of the technology, allowing values like privacy, transparency and accountability to be baked in early (Coates et al., 2022). This is extremely important, regardless of the technology.

The cost, both fiscal and reputational, of rolling back on technology for lack of foresight and tight governance is often staggering. Stories of openly racist, sexist and ableist AI models are on the rise. Meta was recently caught encoding some very bizarre rules for its AI chatbot, including allowing '"sensual" conversations with children' (Prada, 2025). Organisations and governments need to be extremely careful about the way they roll out technology, particularly in a world where societal frustrations are at an all-time high.

Governmental action

In terms of government action, some steps are already visible. Cybersecurity agencies have begun updating guidelines to prepare for quantum threats. Export control regulations now list certain quantum technologies as sensitive, to prevent proliferation to hostile actors.

At the international level, diplomatic dialogues on emerging technologies have included quantum computing on the agenda. While concrete agreements are still forthcoming, we may eventually see something much like an international Quantum Charter or amendments to existing digital treaties that incorporate quantum considerations.

Ethical and safe quantum computing by design: What's being done?

- **Developing guidelines:** Research consortia and ethics institutes are publishing white papers on quantum computing ethics. These documents propose principles such as 'do no harm' in quantum software, transparency in algorithm design, and security by design. While not binding, they influence practitioners and may inform future policy.
- **Collaborative governance:** As mentioned, the World Economic Forum's initiative brings together experts across sectors to discuss governance. This kind of collaboration helps build consensus on thorny issues (e.g., how to verify the integrity of quantum computations, or how to ensure global access) and can lead to voluntary frameworks. It's a proactive approach, trying to shape norms before commercial quantum computing fully arrives (Coates et al., 2022).
- **Regulatory sandboxes:** A few countries are considering sandboxes for quantum tech – controlled environments where companies and researchers can test quantum applications under regulatory supervision. This approach, used previously in fintech, allows authorities to learn about the technology hands on and develop informed rules without stifling innovation.

- **Public awareness and stakeholder engagement:** Some governments and universities have started outreach (workshops, education modules) to demystify quantum computing for nonexperts. A better-informed public can participate in dialogue about acceptable uses of quantum (for instance, weighing surveillance benefits against privacy risks if quantum sensors improve national security). Involving diverse stakeholders, including civil society, in discussions about quantum policy helps capture a wider range of values and concerns.

Ethical considerations are being taken seriously in parallel with technical development. The space is ever evolving, so be on the lookout for emerging best practices around quantum computing, and if you're in cybersecurity, then you might want to specifically seek guidelines on how to handle sensitive data in quantum experiments or recommendations to use open and peer-reviewed quantum algorithms to enhance transparency. Staying abreast of these types of conversations, and contributing where possible, will likely become part and parcel of tech professional roles in the quantum era.

The community is attempting to be proactive by embedding ethics and governance into quantum computing now, so that as quantum computing matures, it does so in a way that aligns with social value and avoids harm. This is absolutely a space for all to be involved in. That means you too!

WORKFORCE IMPLICATIONS AND DIVERSITY CHALLENGES

Realising the potential of quantum computing requires diversity of skill and diversity of people. Currently, the demand for quantum-literate professionals far exceeds the supply, leading to a significant talent shortage. Within that very small pool of talent is an even smaller spread of diverse perspectives.

The talent shortage

A report by McKinsey & Company found that, on average, there is only one qualified candidate for every three quantum computing job openings (Morrison, 2023). In other words, about two-thirds of quantum roles cannot be filled due to the skills shortage. The same analysis projected that fewer than half of all quantum computing jobs will be filled by 2025 if current training rates continued (Morrison, 2023).

This gap spans multiple types of roles: quantum researchers (with deep physics or maths expertise), engineers to build and maintain quantum hardware, software developers who understand quantum algorithms, and even product managers and patent attorneys who grasp quantum fundamentals. The multidisciplinary nature of quantum technology, sitting at the intersection of physics, computer science and mathematics, makes finding qualified people a particular challenge.

The shortage of talent has prompted both industry and academia to ramp up education and training initiatives. Universities are adding courses and specialised programmes in quantum computing. Not too long ago, only a handful of institutions offered degrees in quantum information science; now we're seeing a significant increase in top universities which have master's or PhD tracks dedicated to quantum technology, and more undergraduate programmes include introductory quantum computing modules. These efforts are reflective of the global recognition that quantum literacy must be cultivated across disciplines.

Governments are also heavily investing in quantum skills. For example, the UK National Quantum Technologies Programme (a £1 billion+ initiative) lists the skills gap as a key priority and is funding new centres for doctoral training, as well as exploring apprenticeships in quantum engineering (Morrison, 2023). In the US, the National Science Foundation and Department of Energy have established Quantum Science summer schools and fellowships to grow the talent pipeline, and similar efforts exist in Canada, the EU, China and elsewhere.

Companies are contributing by offering resources to broaden the base of practitioners. IBM's Quantum Experience platform (launched in 2016) and its open source Qiskit framework allow students and developers worldwide to learn quantum programming and even run experiments on real quantum hardware via the cloud (Morrison, 2023). Critically, IBM's Qiskit has reached over 550,000 users globally,[1] and relies on users to translate documentation for other communities,[2] making this a great example of collaboration.

Other firms like Google, Microsoft and startup hubs have sponsored hackathons, coding challenges and free online courses to spark interest and retrain software engineers in quantum concepts. This signals a massive global push to ensure that the workforce can catch up with the technology's advance – because advance it will, and we must ensure we are ready for it.

Equality, diversity and inclusion

The workforce discussion would be incomplete without mentioning equality, diversity and inclusion (EDI) in the quantum computing field. EDI is a hot topic of conversation right now, and opinions on its benefits are extremely polarising; whether you agree or disagree with one side or the other, the fact remains that quantum computing urgently needs skilled professionals from diverse backgrounds. In technology, EDI ensures that innovation reflects the needs and values of all communities.

Like many areas of STEM, quantum computing currently does not reflect the broader population in its demographics. This is largely due to the pipeline issues in feeder disciplines (physics, computer science, engineering), which have historically underrepresented women and other minoritised groups.

---

1 newsroom.ibm.com/2024-05-15-IBM-Expands-Qiskit,-Worlds-Most-Performant-Quantum-Software

2 medium.com/qiskit/we-need-your-help-translating-the-qiskit-textbook-5322453bd7ee

Take the UK for example; around 19% of undergraduates starting computing degrees in 2024 were female (Chartered Institute for IT (BCS), 2024). The ratio of men to women in computing programmes was about 4.1 to 1 in 2024, improved from 5.5 to 1 a few years earlier, but still indicating a large gender gap (Chartered Institute for IT (BCS), 2024).

A recent *Nature* feature noted that only 1 in 54 applicants for quantum jobs is a woman, and that about 80% of quantum technology companies have no women in senior leadership positions (Heidt, 2024).

Preliminary evidence suggests significant underrepresentation of ethnic minorities and economically disadvantaged groups in the quantum sector, though detailed data sources are scarce (Heidt, 2024). Improved data collection is essential in order to track progress and guide interventions.

This matters not only for reasons of equity but also for innovation capacity. Studies in technology and business consistently find that diverse teams are more innovative and effective at solving complex problems. In a cutting-edge field like quantum computing, a homogeneous group might fall victim to 'group think' or could inadvertently design technologies that don't consider the needs and perspectives of large portions of society.

This isn't just tokenistic. Bringing together professionals from all walks of life, backgrounds, disciplines and lived experience can ensure that the technology developed is more universally applicable. More practically, with such a severe talent shortage, *not* tapping into women in tech and various other underrepresented communities is a huge missed opportunity.

It's important to be realistic about this, though. There are likely many voices in the world who would relish the opportunity to join this talent pool, but there are intrinsic societal barriers to inclusion faced by huge swathes of the population. Whether it be apathy, historic mistrust in the system, imposter syndrome or accessibility concerns, it is incumbent on the tech community to build trust and improve how we offer these opportunities to everyone in the fairest way possible.

Reducing inequity and exclusion

- **Investment in education:** To increase the overall supply of talent, education systems are incorporating quantum topics earlier. Some high-school curricula now touch on basic quantum principles (to inspire interest), and interdisciplinary university courses make quantum computing accessible to students in computer science or engineering who might not have a heavy physics background. Online education is playing a big role, with platforms like Coursera and edX offering affordable courses on quantum computing basics, making the field reachable to motivated learners worldwide.
- **Industry training and certification:** Companies and nonprofits are providing pathways for current professionals to transition into quantum. For example, IBM offers a Quantum Developer Certification exam to help IT professionals validate their quantum programming skills. Startups and research labs offer internships or quantum engineer training programmes targeting those with a classical software or hardware background, giving them hands-on experience to pivot careers. By retraining existing tech workers, these programmes can quickly expand the talent pool.
- **Global talent initiatives:** Recognising that expertise is scarce, some countries are actively attracting quantum talent from abroad (through special visas or research grants) and fostering international collaboration. Global research projects, such as EU-funded networks or bilateral agreements (e.g., between the US and Japan on quantum research), facilitate the exchange of researchers and students. This not only facilitates the cross-pollination of highly sought after knowledge but also builds personal connections that might encourage experts to move where opportunities are, somewhat easing talent distribution issues.

- **Encouraging diversity:** To improve representation, targeted efforts are being made at multiple levels. Scholarships and fellowships for women and minorities in quantum-related fields aim to remove financial barriers. Mentorship programmes like 'Women in Quantum' provide support and role models for early-career women in the field. Conferences and journals are starting to track diversity metrics and host panels on inclusivity in quantum technology.

  Some companies have set concrete diversity hiring goals for their quantum teams or are partnering with universities that serve underrepresented populations to recruit interns. An interesting point from the community is that since quantum computing is relatively new, it's an opportunity to get things right early on in building an inclusive culture, rather than trying to fix an established culture later (Heidt, 2024). In other words, many leaders are aware of the historic lack of diversity in physics and are actively trying to avoid simply replicating that in the quantum sector (Heidt, 2024).

- **Inclusive workplace culture:** Beyond recruitment, retention is critical. Companies and research institutions are looking at how to create environments where diverse talent thrives. This includes measures like flexible work policies (important for those with caregiving responsibilities, for instance), clear anti-harassment stances, and providing networking opportunities for minority groups in the field. There are also efforts such as unconscious bias training for managers in quantum tech firms, to ensure evaluations and promotions are fair. Notably, several prominent women in quantum computing have founded or joined advocacy groups to keep diversity on the agenda and celebrate achievements of underrepresented groups, which helps in visibility and morale.

The quantum computing boom needs talented individuals and is creating opportunities for a wide range of skillsets. For IT professionals that have a background in software, engineering or maths, there are increasing resources to help gain quantum knowledge and potentially enter this field. It is no longer a necessary requirement to have a PhD in quantum physics.

As the industry grows, it needs engineers, coders, project managers and others who can bridge between quantum specialists and real-world applications. At the same time, being aware of diversity challenges means the diligent IT professional can support initiatives for inclusion, whether that's mentoring newcomers from underrepresented groups or simply fostering a respectful team culture. A more diverse workforce isn't just a nice idea, it could directly contribute to better technology and a more inclusive community

ECONOMIC AND GEOPOLITICAL IMPLICATIONS

Quantum computing has quickly become a geostrategic priority on the global stage. Nations and corporations view quantum technology as a potential panacea for challenges in drug discovery, climate modelling and cybersecurity, and this is fuelling economic competitiveness and national security concerns alike. This has led to what some describe as a global quantum race, echoing past technological scrambles like the nuclear arms race or, slightly less threateningly, the Cold War space race.

The race for quantum advantage

A central concern is whether one country (or a small group of countries) achieves a major quantum computing breakthrough, namely a large-scale, general-purpose quantum computer, well ahead of others. The implications of such a head start could be far-reaching.

From an economic perspective, a country that leads in quantum computing would capture significant value across various industries. Quantum breakthroughs may catalyse new markets and make existing industries more efficient. For example, quantum computers could vastly improve drug discovery by simulating molecular interactions that are too complex for classical computers, potentially giving the leading country a competitive edge in pharmaceuticals and healthcare (Hidary and Sarkar, 2023).

Similarly, quantum-powered algorithms could be used to great effect in logistics and finance by solving complex routing and risk analysis problems much faster, benefiting sectors like transportation and banking (Hidary and Sarkar, 2023). A nation at the forefront might see an influx of investment and talent, much like Silicon Valley benefited from being the early centre of classical computing; thus, early leaders in quantum may attract disproportionate investment and talent.

Intellectual property in quantum technologies (patents on hardware designs, algorithms etc.) could become lucrative assets that reinforce a country's economic lead; however, this concentration may stifle innovation or create monopolistic dynamics. Indeed, as of 2022, global public spending on quantum R&D was estimated to exceed $30 billion, but around 75% of that was from just a handful of big players (China alone accounting for roughly half, the EU about a quarter, and the remainder primarily from the US, Canada, Japan and the UK; Hidary and Sarkar, 2023). This concentration of investment suggests that those making the earliest big bets expect a sizeable payoff in terms of economic influence.

These benefits will not be evenly distributed by default. We can already observe a concerning quantum divide: as noted earlier, only 17 out of 150 countries have active quantum programmes (Hidary and Sarkar, 2023). If this divide persists or widens, it could exacerbate global inequalities.

The global quantum divide

Countries without quantum capabilities might become reliant on those that have them, whether that means buying services from foreign quantum providers or simply lagging in technological productivity. For example, nations lacking quantum capabilities may struggle to compete in materials science, where quantum simulations accelerate innovation.

A World Economic Forum analysis pointed out that unequal access to quantum tech has negative geopolitical implications, potentially causing less-advanced countries to fall further behind in economic and security terms (Hidary and Sarkar, 2023). This scenario is analogous to the digital divide of the internet age (where some populations benefited from connectivity while others were left out), but the stakes could be even higher if critical infrastructure and national economies are affected by who does or doesn't have quantum capabilities.

National security

In terms of national security and geopolitical power, the distribution of quantum computing expertise could shift the balance of intelligence and military capabilities. A frequently cited example is cryptography: a country with superior quantum computing could decrypt other nations' sensitive communications that were once considered secure (Hidary and Sarkar, 2023; Swayne, 2025).

US Homeland Security has also warned that current encryption standards might be defeated by 2030 with a quantum computer (Hidary and Sarkar, 2023). If one nation achieves that first, it would gain a significant intelligence advantage, potentially able to eavesdrop on others' diplomatic cables, military communications or financial transactions. This has been described as a new kind of arms race, where the 'weapon' is computational power rather than firepower.

Beyond code breaking, quantum technologies include extremely precise sensors and quantum communication networks. Those could be used, for example, to detect submarines or stealth aircraft, or to create communication links that are secure against eavesdropping (using quantum key distribution).

A country that can master these applications could offset some of its opponents' advantages. It's easy to see why defence departments across the globe are investing in quantum research: no one wants to be caught flat-footed if an adversary suddenly has a strategic tech edge.

Global collaboration / progressive realism in quantum computing

In all probability, the likelihood of a permanent quantum monopoly by a single country is quite low. Historically, in transformative technologies, initial leads (like the US in early computing or the Soviet Union in space) spurred others to catch up, often rapidly. Knowledge tends to diffuse, and talent flows to where opportunities are, so others eventually narrow the gap. This is where the lens of progressive realism can be especially advantageous.

Progressive realism is a foreign policy paradigm that advocates meeting progressive goals using realist means. Foremost in this is an acceptance of the world as it is: volatile, uncertain, complex and ambiguous (VUCA). In the context of quantum computing, the goal isn't simply winning the quantum advantage race, but instead ensuring the equitable distribution of access to technology, knowledge and benefits among nations and communities. The long-term goal is to reap as many benefits from quantum computing as possible, while avoiding as much of the negative impact as possible.

We're already seeing international spread; for example, while the US and China started strongly in quantum computing, countries like Canada, Australia and Germany have built strong programmes and startups, and even smaller nations like Finland, Israel and Singapore have carved out niches. However, even a temporary lead of a few years could confer significant advantages in the interim, which is why the race is intense. No major power wants to be years behind its rivals in such a pivotal area.

There are also cooperation scenarios that could mitigate some competitive tensions. Scientific collaboration doesn't necessarily stop at borders; many quantum research results are published openly and involve cross-country coauthors. For example, the development of quantum-resistant encryption is a global effort (researchers from multiple countries contributed to the algorithms chosen by NIST), because it's in everyone's interest to secure data; this is a case where countries are working together despite competition elsewhere.

Additionally, some regions form alliances: the European Union pools resources among member states, and there are joint projects like the Quantum Communication Partnership between certain nations to build secure networks collectively.

There is a clear intent to improve cooperation among nations in order to share the benefits of quantum technology and accelerate the rate at which we can reap them. As with most other advances in technology, this may include a period of tension or instability, which is why designing ethical and equitable rollouts is more crucial than ever.

Addressing gaps and tension in response to quantum computing

- **National quantum strategies:** To avoid falling behind, many countries are developing their own quantum strategies (if they haven't already). As of 2023, at least 20 countries had some form of strategy or significant initiative, and more are following (Hidary and Sarkar, 2023). These plans typically involve funding research, building quantum education programmes and fostering startups. For countries late to the party, some focus on niche strengths – for example, a nation might specialise in quantum sensing (if it has a strong precision instrument industry) or in certain software applications. Broadly, this mitigates the monopoly scenario by ensuring multiple centres of quantum progress.
- **Global collaboration:** International collaboration is being encouraged in areas that benefit all. One example is the OpenQuantum Initiative, a loose movement urging that some quantum software and tools remain open source so that everyone can access them, not just the richest companies. Another example is scientific conferences and organisations explicitly reaching out to researchers from underrepresented regions to include them in projects. The underlying idea is that quantum computing,

like climate science or space exploration, can also be an arena of cooperation where shared goals (like improving healthcare or tackling climate modelling with quantum simulations) bring nations together.

- **Talent and knowledge sharing:** Some mitigation of the divide comes from human capital exchange. Leading countries are offering scholarships and positions to students and scientists from other countries, for instance bringing in students from Africa or Southeast Asia (where quantum programmes are nascent) to train in US or European labs. Those individuals might become quantum ambassadors, helping start efforts in their home countries later. Organisations such as the International Centre for Theoretical Physics have workshops aimed at scientists from developing nations to get up to speed on quantum information science, trying to seed expertise more widely.
- **Agreements on responsible use:** To address the security dilemma (where everyone fears others' quantum capabilities), there are early talks about norms or agreements on quantum computing use. For instance, one proposal is that countries could mutually agree not to target each other's critical infrastructure with quantum attacks (much as there are norms against attacking civilian infrastructure in conventional war). While formal treaties are still hypothetical, including quantum topics in cybersecurity dialogues (like those under the UN or between NATO and other powers) at least acknowledges the issue. A parallel can be drawn with how countries agreed to some norms for cyberspace and AI – it often starts with nonbinding norms that could later become formal agreements.
- **Inclusivity in economic benefits:** On the economic front, there's advocacy for thinking about quantum tech in development agendas. The idea is that international development organisations (like the World Bank or regional development banks) could fund some quantum technology projects in developing countries, or help create partnerships between tech-leading countries

and lower-income ones (for example, using quantum sensing for agriculture or water management in Africa, in collaboration with European researchers). This way, some benefits of the quantum revolution could reach the Global South sooner, and those countries also start building capacity by working on applied projects that matter to them.

Keeping your eye on the quantum landscape is a good idea. As quantum computing breaks over the tipping point, the opportunities for career moves will likely be bountiful. Industries like finance and pharmaceuticals are already exploring quantum solutions, so those with both domain knowledge and quantum literacy may be in great demand.

Quantum computing is not developing in a political vacuum; it's increasingly seen as a national priority akin to past strategic technologies. This dynamic is driving massive investment and some competitive behaviour, but there are also massive efforts to ensure it doesn't turn into a stark divide of haves and have-nots.

The outcome will likely be a mix of competition and collaboration – a race, but one hopefully tempered by the understanding that certain quantum-enabled threats (like broken encryption) harm everyone, and certain advances (like cures for diseases) help everyone. Navigating this landscape will require technical experts to also be savvy about policy and international context, a convergence that is already evident in the way governments are hiring quantum advisors and companies are lobbying on quantum policies.

CONCLUSION

For IT professionals just starting to follow this field, don't worry, there's a lot to learn and even more to ponder on. Simply approaching these large and complex ethical and geopolitical discussions can be helpful in formulating ideas where they can contribute. Regardless of whether it's in crafting secure software, educating others or participating in policy discussions, the world will invariably need quantum-literate professionals – and soon! Short of growing them in labs, we must look to professionals in the community today, regardless of background, to fill these gaps and make use of the significant investment that sectors are pouring into upskilling them.

As this technology evolves, a well-informed and engaged IT community will be essential to ensure that the quantum leap is one that society is ready to take. Staying aware of the ethical, workforce, geopolitical and security dimensions discussed in this chapter, you will not only be better prepared for the changes quantum computing may bring, but can also play a part in guiding those changes towards positive outcomes.

FURTHER READING

Further reading on the topics raised in this chapter can be found in Ivezic (2024, 2025) and Quantum Zeitgeist (2024).

8 THE QUANTUM FUTURE

Jeremy Green

INTRODUCTION

Throughout this book, we have explored the foundations of quantum computing, the risks it poses to cryptography and the solutions, particularly PQC, that will protect us. But what does the future actually hold? When will quantum computers arrive? How will they change our world? And what should we be doing now to prepare?

This final chapter looks ahead at hardware roadmaps, realistic timelines and the broader societal impact of the quantum revolution. It also addresses a fundamental question posed by Richard Feynman over four decades ago. If nature is quantum, should our computers be too?

FEYNMAN'S VISION: SIMULATING NATURE WITH NATURE

In 1981, the physicist Richard Feynman delivered a lecture that would become foundational to quantum computing (Feynman, 1982). He observed that classical computers struggle immensely to simulate quantum systems – the behaviour of atoms, molecules and particles. The reason is simple: quantum systems exhibit superposition and entanglement, creating an exponential complexity that classical machines cannot handle.

Feynman's insight was profound and elegant: the only way to efficiently simulate a quantum system is with another, controllable, quantum system. He was not proposing a general-purpose computer in the way we think of them today. He was suggesting that if we want to understand nature at its most fundamental level, we need tools that speak nature's language.

This vision has guided quantum computing ever since. Today's quantum processors, however limited, are the first steps toward realising Feynman's dream of using quantum mechanics to explore quantum mechanics. The irony, of course, is that these same machines, built to understand the universe, may also break the cryptographic systems that secure our digital world.

ANALOGUE CORE

In computing, an analogue core refers to the part of a system where computation is performed using continuous physical quantities rather than digital ones and zeros. It is the continuous-signal heart of a computing architecture (see Figure 8.1): the region where voltages, currents, mechanical motion, optical fields or other physical phenomena directly model the mathematical behaviour of a system. This aligns with the definition of analogue computing, where physical processes evolve continuously to represent and solve equations.

Figure 8.1 Analogue core

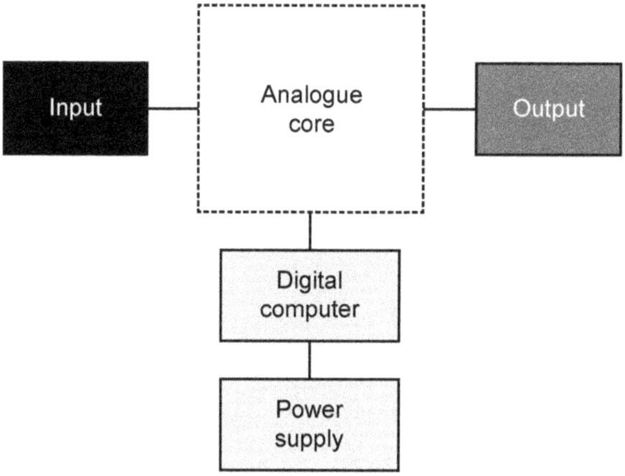

The quantum computers most people read about, such as IBM's superconducting processors or Google's Sycamore, are digital (or gate-based) quantum computers. They operate using quantum logic gates, analogously to how classical computers use logic gates. Qubits are manipulated through discrete operations, and algorithms like Shor's are expressed as circuits. This approach is general purpose; a large enough, fault-tolerant digital quantum computer could run any quantum algorithm, including those that break public-key cryptography.

Analogue core computers work differently. Instead of applying discrete gates, they are programmed by carefully controlling the physical Hamiltonian (the energy landscape) of a quantum system. The system then naturally evolves from an initial state to a final state that encodes the solution to a problem.

The most prominent and commercially successful example is quantum annealing, pioneered by D-Wave Systems. An annealer starts in a simple, low-energy state and slowly transitions to a problem Hamiltonian. Quantum tunnelling allows the system to escape local minima and find global optima. This is exceptionally powerful for a specific class of optimisation problems.

Analogue systems are easier to build than fault-tolerant digital machines. D-Wave has been selling commercial annealers since 2011. Organisations are already using them and their hybrid classical quantum solvers to tackle complex optimisation problems in logistics, supply chain management, financial modelling and materials science. This means the commercial and industrial impact of quantum computing is arriving through analogue systems, years before a digital machine will ever factor a large prime.

The Feynman connection

Interestingly, analogue quantum computing is closer to Feynman's original vision than the gate-based approach. Feynman spoke of simulating physics with physics – letting one quantum system naturally evolve to mimic another. Analogue systems do exactly this. They are not universal in the

Turing sense, but they are exquisitely tailored to the problems Feynman cared about most.

THE PATH TO FAULT-TOLERANT QUANTUM COMPUTING

The quantum computers that exist today are called NISQ devices (see Chapter 1). They have enough qubits (typically 50–500) to demonstrate quantum advantage for specific problems, but they are not yet fault tolerant. Errors accumulate and coherence is limited, so running deep algorithms like Shor's is impossible.

The next great milestone is fault-tolerant quantum computing machines capable of correcting errors faster than they occur, allowing arbitrarily long computations. This requires millions of physical qubits working together to form thousands of logical, error-corrected qubits.

Major players have published roadmaps toward this goal:

- **IBM** aims to build its first fault-tolerant quantum computer by 2029. The 'Starling' system is designed to deliver 200 logical qubits and execute 100 million fault-tolerant operations. While 200 logical qubits are below the ~4000 needed for RSA-2048 factoring, IBM's roadmap implies rapid scaling thereafter.
- **Google Quantum AI** has demonstrated that scaling surface-code logical qubits reduces error rates – a critical milestone. Their 'Willow' processor shows exponential improvement in fidelity with logical qubit growth. Google could reach the required ~4000 logical qubits with sufficient throughput by 2030–2032.
- **QuEra** uses neutral-atom technology, which offers flexible two- and three-dimensional arrays with natural scalability. Their Gemini processor operates with ~260 physical qubits and gate fidelities around 99.5%. Projections suggest QuEra could approach 1,000–1,200 logical qubits by 2032, potentially crossing into CRQC readiness.

The CRQC Readiness Benchmark and Q-Day

To make sense of these different roadmaps, researchers have developed tools to compare progress toward cryptanalytically relevant quantum computing. The CRQC Readiness Benchmark (q-day.org) provides a structured way to estimate when a quantum computer could break RSA-2048.

The benchmark considers three dimensions:

- **logical qubit capacity** (LQC): the number of error-corrected logical qubits available;
- **logical operations budget** (LOB): the maximum number of fault-tolerant operations executable before decoherence;
- **quantum operations throughput** (QOT): the sustained rate of logical operations per second.

A CRQC score of 1.0 corresponds to the practical capability to factor RSA-2048 within one week.

When we apply these metrics to vendor roadmaps:

- **IBM** (2029): Targets ~200 logical qubits with LDPC error correction.[1]
- **Google** (2030–2032): Willow processor scaling to ~1,400 logical qubits, yielding a CRQC score of 1.4, comfortably above the breakability threshold.[2]
- **QuEra** (2032 optimistic): Neutral-atom arrays projected at ~1,000 logical qubits, with CRQC score 0.64, approaching but not yet at threshold.
- **QuEra** (2032 breakthrough): With ~1,200 logical qubits and full throughput, gets a CRQC score of 1.2, crossing into CRQC readiness.

1 ibm.com/quantum/roadmap

2 quantumai.google

Taken together, these projections suggest Q-Day, the point at which RSA-2048 can be broken in under a week, could arrive as early as 2029 and is likely by 2032.

THE Y2K COMPARISON AND WHY IT'S WRONG

Some dismiss the quantum risk as 'another Y2K', a problem that generated immense hype but ultimately passed with minimal disruption. This comparison is dangerously misleading.

Y2K had a fixed deadline of midnight, 1 January 2000. The world knew exactly when the problem would manifest and a coordinated global effort ensured systems were patched in time. The absence of catastrophe was not because the threat was overblown, but because thousands of engineers worked tirelessly to prevent it.

Q-Day has no fixed date. No press release will announce that RSA has finally fallen. Adversaries will not declare their success; they will simply begin decrypting the data they have been harvesting for years. The problem is invisible, the deadline unknown and the consequence not a system crash but a silent, massive data breach.

WORKFORCE AND SOCIETAL IMPACT

Quantum computing will not only break cryptography, it will transform industries, create new jobs and render others obsolete. The quantum workforce is desperately small. There are simply not enough people who understand both quantum mechanics and cybersecurity to manage the coming transition. This creates both a challenge and an opportunity:

- Cryptographers are needed to analyse and implement PQC algorithms.
- Security architects must redesign systems for crypto-agility.

- Risk managers must integrate quantum threats into enterprise frameworks.
- Developers must learn to use PQC libraries and avoid implementation flaws.
- Executives must understand enough to prioritise quantum readiness.

Universities are scrambling to expand quantum programmes, but the pipeline takes years. In the meantime, organisations must upskill existing staff and compete for scarce talent, as outlined in point 2 of Cryptomathic (2026).

Industry transformation

Beyond security, quantum computing promises breakthroughs in:

- **drug discovery:** simulating molecular interactions to design new medicines;
- **materials science:** developing better batteries, solar cells and superconductors;
- **optimisation:** solving logistics, supply chain and financial modelling problems;
- **artificial intelligence:** accelerating machine learning and pattern recognition.

The countries and companies that lead in quantum will gain enormous economic and strategic advantages. Those that lag will become dependent on others for critical capabilities.

The digital divide

There is a real risk of a quantum divide, with nations and organisations with quantum capabilities pulling away from those without. This mirrors the digital divide of the 1990s but is steeper and more consequential. Quantum advantage in computation translates directly into advantage in intelligence, economic competition and military capability.

For smaller organisations, the path may be different. Some will wait for cloud providers and software vendors to build PQC into the products they use. Others will replace legacy systems only when forced to by compliance or a breach. This creates a two-speed world: the quantum-ready and the quantum-vulnerable.

CONCLUSION

Quantum computing is an engineering challenge with people around the world solving issues around scaling up, year by year, qubit by qubit. The machines that will break RSA are being designed today. The data that will be decrypted is being collected today. The decisions that determine whether an organisation is ready are being made today.

Richard Feynman understood that to simulate nature, we must think like nature. The quantum future will be built by those who understand that principle and act on it with purpose. The question is not whether quantum computers will arrive. The question is whether we will be ready when they do.

For those who prepare, the quantum era offers extraordinary opportunities of new science, new industries, new capabilities. For those who wait, it offers only uncertainty of breached data, broken trust and the slow realisation that the future arrived while their budget was spent on AI with a reduced IT upgrade and security budget.

FURTHER READING

Further reading around these topics is available from the NIST Post-Quantum Cryptography Project[3] and Keyfactor Quantum Readiness Resources.[4]

---

3 csrc.nist.gov/projects/post-quantum-cryptography

4 keyfactor.com/resources/quantum-readiness/

REFERENCES

Aaronson, S. (2013) *Quantum Computing since Democritus*. Cambridge: Cambridge University Press. doi.org/10.1017/CBO9780511979309

Aharonov, D., van Dam, W., Kempe, J., Landau, Z., Lloyd, S., and Regev, O. (2004) Adiabatic quantum computation is equivalent to standard quantum computation. In *Proceedings of the 45th Annual IEEE Symposium on Foundations of Computer Science (FOCS '04)*. IEEE Computer Society. 42–51. doi.org/10.1109/FOCS.2004.8

Aquina, N., Cimoli, B., Das, S., Hövelmanns, K., Weber, F. J., Okonkwo, C., Rommel, S., Škorić, B., Monroy, I. T., and Verschoor, S. (2025) A critical analysis of deployed use cases for quantum key distribution and comparison with post-quantum cryptography. *EPJ Quantum Technology*, 12 (1). 51. doi.org/10.1140/epjqt/s40507-025-00350-5

Ausiello, G., Crescenzi, P., Gambosi, G., Kann, V., Marchetti-Spaccamela, A., and Protasi, M. (1999) *Complexity and Approximation: Combinatorial Optimization Problems and Their Approximability Properties*. Berlin: Springer. doi.org/10.1007/978-3-642-58412-1

Barahona, F., Grötschel, M., Jünger, M., and Reinelt, G. (1988) An application of combinatorial optimization to statistical physics and circuit layout design. *Operations Research*, 36 (3). 493–513. doi.org/10.1287/opre.36.3.493

Bennett, C. H., and Brassard, G. (1984) Quantum cryptography: Public key distribution and coin tossing. In *Proceedings of the IEEE International Conference on Computers, Systems and Signal Processing*. Bangalore, 10–12 December 1984. IEEE. 175–179.

Bennett, C. H., Brassard, G., and Mermin, N. D. (1992) Quantum cryptography without Bell's theorem. *Physical Review Letters*, 68. 557. doi.org/10.1103/PhysRevLett.68.557

Bernardini, F., Chakraborty, A., and Ordóñez, C. R. (2024) Quantum computing with trapped ions: A beginner's guide, *European Journal of Physics*, 45. 013001. doi.org/10.1088/1361-6404/ad06be

Bindel, N., Brendel, J., Fischlin, M., Goncalves, B., and Stebila, D. (2019) Hybrid key encapsulation mechanisms and authenticated key exchange. In J. Ding and R. Steinwandt (eds). *Post-Quantum Cryptography*. Cham: Springer. 206–226.

Bluvstein, D., et al. (2022) A quantum processor based on coherent transport of entangled atom arrays. *Nature*, 604 (7906). 451–456. doi.org/10.1038/s41586-022-04592-6

Bolgar, C. (2025) Microsoft's Majorana 1 chip carves new path for quantum computing. Microsoft. Available from: https://news.microsoft.com/source/features/innovation/microsofts-majorana-1-chip-carves-new-path-for-quantum-computing/

Brain, M. J., Crick, T., Fitch, J. P., and De Vos, M. (2006) An application of answer set programming: Superoptimisation (a preliminary report). Technical Report CSBU-2006-05, University of Bath.

Brassard, G., Høyer, P., and Tapp, A. (1998) Quantum algorithm for the collision problem. In *Proceedings of the Third Latin American Symposium on Theoretical Informatics (LATIN'98)*. Berlin: Springer. 163–169.

Braunstein, S. L., and Van Loock, P. (2005) Quantum information with continuous variables. *Reviews of Modern Physics*, 77 (2). 513–577. doi.org/10.1103/RevModPhys.77.513

Brierley, S. (2025) Quantum error correction, theory → technology. vimeo.com/1104057419/5d5bc93fbd.

Browaeys, A., Barredo, D., and Lahaye, T. (2016) Experimental investigations of dipole–dipole interactions between a few Rydberg atoms. *Journal of Physics B: Atomic, Molecular and Optical Physics*, 49 (15). 152001. doi.org/10.1088/0953-4075/49/15/152001

Buchanan, W. J. (2024) A long goodbye to RSA and ECDSA, and quick hello to SLH-DSA. Medium. Available at https://medium.com/asecuritysite-when-bob-met-alice/a-long-goodbye-to-rsa-and-ecdsa-and-quick-hello-to-slh-dsa-3e53e36a941b.

Calégari, P., Guidec, F., Kuonen, P., and Nielsen, F. (2001) Combinatorial optimization algorithms for radio network planning. *Theoretical Computer Science*, 263 (1–2). 235–245. doi.org/10.1016/S0304-3975(00)00245-0

Cerf, N. J., Adami, C., and Kwiat, P. G. (1998) Optical simulation of quantum logic. *Physical Review A*, 57 (3). R1477. doi.org/10.1103/PhysRevA.57.R1477

Chartered Institute for IT (BCS) (2024) Female computing students closed the gap on men in 2024 – new data shows. BCS. Available from: bcs.org/articles-opinion-and-research/female-computing-students-closed-the-gap-on-men-in-2024-new-data-shows/ [15 August 2024].

Chen, L., Jordan, S., Liu, Y., Moody, D., Peralta, R., Perlner, R., and Smith-Tone, D. (2016) *Report on post-quantum cryptography*. Gaithersburg, MD: National Institute of Standards and Technology. Available from: nvlpubs.nist.gov/nistpubs/ir/2016/NIST.IR.8105.pdf [15 August 2025].

Coates, R., et al. (2022). *Quantum computing governance principles*. World Economic Forum. Available from: www3.weforum.org/docs/WEF_Quantum_Computing_2022.pdf [16 August 2025].

Connolly, D., Barnes, R., and Grubbs, P. (2026a) Hybrid post-quantum key encapsulation mechanisms. IRTF draft proposal. Available from: datatracker.ietf.org/doc/draft-irtf-cfrg-hybrid-kems

Connolly, D., Ounsworth, M., Schmieg, S., and Stebila, D. (2026b) StarHunters: Secure hybrid post-quantum KEMs from IND-CCA2 PKEs. Cryptology ePrint archive. eprint.iacr.org/2026/427

Cook, J., Eidenbenz, S., and Bärtschi, A. (2020) The quantum alternating operator ansatz on maximum *k*-vertex cover. In *Proceedings 2020 IEEE International Conference on Quantum Computing and Engineering (QCE)*. IEEE. 83–92. doi.org/10.1109/QCE49297.2020.00021

Cryptomathic (2026) *A banker's guide to quantum safe cryptography part 2: Roadblocks to PQC migration and strategic solutions for financial institutions*. Cryptomathic. Available at: cryptomathic.com/blog/a-bankers-guide-to-quantum-safe-cryptography-part-2 [31 March 2026].

Daemen, J., and Rijmen, V. (2020) *The Design of Rijndael: The Advanced Encryption Standard (AES)*, 2nd edn. Berlin: Springer.

Davenport, J. H., and Pring, B. I. (2021) Improvements to quantum search techniques for block-ciphers, with applications to AES. In Dunkelman, O., Jacobson Jr., M. J., and O'Flynn, C. (eds). *Selected Areas in Cryptography*. Berlin: Springer. 360–384. doi.org/10.1007/978-3-030-81652-0_14

Deutsch, D., and Jozsa, R. (1992) Rapid solution of problems by quantum computation. *Proceedings of the Royal Society of London. Series A*, 439 (1907). 553–558. doi.org/10.1098/rspa.1992.0167

Diffie, W., and Hellman, M. E. (1976) New directions in cryptography. *IEEE Transactions on Information Theory*, 22 (6). 644–654. doi.org/10.1109/TIT.1976.1055638

Dirac, P. A. M. (1939). A new notation for quantum mechanics. *Mathematical Proceedings of the Cambridge Philosophical Society*, 35. 416–418.

DiVincenzo, D. P. (1997) Topics in quantum computers. In L. S. Sohn, L. P. Kouwenhoven and G. Schön (eds). *Mesoscopic Electron Transport*. Dordrecht: Springer. 657–677. doi.org/10.1007/978-94-015-8839-3_18

DiVincenzo, D. P. (2000) The physical implementation of quantum computation. *Fortschritte der Physik*, 48 (9–11). 771–783. doi.org/10.1002/1521-3978(200009)48:9/11%3C771::AID-PROP771%3E3.0.CO;2-E

Eén, N., and Sörensson, N. (2003) An extensible SAT-solver. In Giunchiglia, E., and Tacchella, A. (eds). *Theory and Applications of Satisfiability Testing*, Berlin: Springer. 502–518. doi.org/10.1007/978-3-540-24605-3_37

Ekert, A. K. (1991) Quantum cryptography based on Bell's theorem. *Physical Review Letters*, 67. 661. doi.org/10.1103/PhysRevLett.67.661

Esposito, A., and Danzig, T. (2024) Hybrid classical-quantum simulation of Maxcut using QAOA-in-QAOA. In *Proceedings 2024 IEEE International Parallel and Distributed Processing Symposium Workshops (IPDPSW)*. IEEE. 1088–1094.

Esposito, A., Jones, J. R., Cabaniols, S., and Brayford, D. (2023) A hybrid classical–quantum HPC workload. In *Proceedings of the 2023 IEEE International Conference on Quantum Computing and Engineering (QCE)*, vol. 2. IEEE. 117–121. doi.org/10.1109/QCE57702.2023.10194

Fall, A. A. (2025) SoK: Systematizing hybrid strategies for the transition to post-quantum cryptography. Cryptology ePrint archive. eprint.iacr.org/2025/2052

Farhi, E., Goldstone, J., and Gutmann, S. (2014). A quantum approximate optimization algorithm. Preprint. arxiv.org/abs/1411.4028

Feynman, R. (1982) Simulating physics with computers. *International Journal of Theoretical Physics*, 21. 467–488. doi.org/10.1007/BF02650179

Gilkolaei, R. R., and Ebrahimi, R. (2025) Quantum resource analysis of low-round Keccak/SHA-3 preimage attack: From classical $2^{57.8}$ to quantum $2^{28.9}$ using Qiskit modeling. Cryptology ePrint archive. eprint.iacr.org/2025/2277

Grover, L. K. (1996) A fast quantum mechanical algorithm for database search. In *Proceedings of the 28th Annual ACM Symposium on the Theory of Computing*. ACM. 212–219. doi.org/10.1145/237814.237866

Hadfield, S., Wang, Z., O'Gorman, B., Rieffel, E. G., Venturelli, D., and Biswas, R. (2019) From the quantum approximate optimization algorithm to a quantum alternating operator ansatz. *Algorithms*, 12 (2). 34. doi.org/10.3390/a12020034

Heidt, A. (2024) Quantum computing aims for diversity, one qubit at a time. *Nature*, 632. 464–465. doi.org/10.1038/d41586-024-02541-z

Hidary, J. D. (2021) *Quantum Computing: An Applied Approach*, 2nd edn. Cham: Springer. doi.org/10.1007/978-3-030-83274-2

Hidary, J., and Sarkar, A. (2023) The world is heading for a 'quantum divide': Here's why it matters. World Economic Forum. Available from: weforum.org/stories/2023/01/the-world-quantum-divide-why-it-matters-davos2023/ [17 August 2025].

Hoefler, T., Häner, T., and Troyer, M. (2023) Disentangling hype from practicality: On realistically achieving quantum advantage. *Communications of the ACM*, 66 (5). 82–87. doi.org/10.1145/3571725

Hülsing, A., Ning, K. C., Schwabe, P., Weber, F. J., and Zimmermann, P. R. (2021) Post-quantum wireguard. In *Proceedings of the 2021 IEEE Symposium on Security and Privacy (SP)*. IEEE Computer Society. 304–321. doi.org/10.1109/SP40001.2021.00030

Ivezic, M. (2024) 4,099 qubits: The myth and reality of breaking RSA 2048 with quantum computers. *Post-Quantum*. Available from: postquantum.com/post-quantum/4099-qubits-rsa/ [15 August 2025].

Ivezic, M. (2025) Q-day revisited – RSA-2048 broken by 2030: Detailed analysis. *Post-Quantum*. Available from: postquantum.com/post-quantum/q-day-y2q-rsa-broken-2030/ [15 August 2025].

Jaksch, D., et al. (2000) Fast quantum gates for neutral atoms. *Physical Review Letters*, 85. 2208. doi.org/10.1103/PhysRevLett.85.2208

Johnson, M. W., et al. (2011) Quantum annealing with manufactured spins. *Nature*, 473 (7346). 194–198. doi.org/10.1038/nature10012

Johnston, E. R., Harrigan, N., and Gimeno-Segovia, M. (2019) *Programming Quantum Computers: Essential Algorithms and Code Samples*. Sebastopol, CA: O'Reilly.

Kadowaki, T., and Nishimori, H. (1998). Quantum annealing in the transverse Ising model. *Physical Review E*, 58 (5). 5355. doi.org/10.1103/PhysRevE.58.5355

Kahana, E. (2020) Quantum computing and AI algorithmic bias. Stanford Law School. Available from: law.stanford.edu/2020/02/06/quantum-computing-and-algorithmic-bias/ [15 August 2025].

Kirkpatrick, S., Gelatt Jr., C. D., and Vecchi, M. P. (1983) Optimization by simulated annealing. *Science*, 220 (4598). 671–680. doi.org/10.1126/science.220.4598.671

Kitaev, A. Y. (1995) Quantum measurements and the Abelian stabilizer problem. Preprint. arxiv.org/abs/quant-ph/9511026

Kjaergaard, M., et al. (2020) Superconducting qubits: Current state of play. *Annual Review of Condensed Matter Physics*, 11. 369–395. doi.org/10.1146/annurev-conmatphys-031119-050605

Knill, E., Laflamme, R., and Milburn, G. J. (2001) A scheme for efficient quantum computation with linear optics. *Nature*, 409 (6816). 46–52. doi.org/10.1038/35051009

Kok, P., Munro, W. J., Nemoto, K., Ralph, T. C., Dowling, J. P., and Milburn, G. J. (2007) Linear optical quantum computing with photonic qubits. *Reviews of Modern Physics*, 79. 135–174. doi.org/10.1103/RevModPhys.79.135

Lenstra, A. K., Lenstra Jr., H. W., Manasse, M. S., and Pollard, J. M. (1993a) The number field sieve. In Lenstra, A. J., and Lenstra, H. W. (eds). *The Development of the Number Field Sieve*. Berlin: Springer. 11–42.

Lenstra, A. K., Lenstra Jr., H. W., Manasse, M. S., and Pollard, J. M. (1993b) The factorisation of the ninth Fermat number. *Mathematics of Computation*, 61 (203). 319–349. doi.org/10.2307/2152957

Lodewijks, B. (2019) Mapping NP-hard and NP-complete optimisation problems to quadratic unconstrained binary optimisation problems. Preprint. arxiv.org/abs/1911.08043

Lucas, A. (2014) Ising formulations of many NP problems. *Frontiers in Physics*, 2. 5. doi.org/10.3389/fphy.2014.00005

Morrison, R. (2023) Quantum computing has a looming skills gap. Tech Monitor. Available from: techmonitor.ai/hardware/quantum/quantum-computing-has-a-looming-skills-gap [17 August 2025].

Mouaji, M., and Al-Kuwari, S. (2026) Multiparty quantum key agreement: Architectures, state-of-the-art, and open problems. Preprint. arxiv.org/abs/2603.03225

Nielsen, M. A. (2006) Cluster-state quantum computation. *Reports on Mathematical Physics*, 57 (1). 147–161. doi.org/10.1016/S0034-4877(06)80014-5

O'Brien, J. L. (2007) Optical quantum computing. *Science*, 318 (5856). 1567–1570. doi.org/10.1126/science.1142892

Pan, F., Chen, K., and Zhang, P. (2022) Solving the sampling problem of the sycamore quantum circuits. *Physical Review Letters*, 129. 090502. doi.org/10.1103/PhysRevLett.129.090502

Pelofske, E., Bärtschi, A., and Eidenbenz, S. (2024) Short-depth QAOA circuits and quantum annealing on higher-order Ising models. *NPJ Quantum Information*, 10 (1). 30. doi.org/10.1038/s41534-024-00825-w

Prada, L. (2025) Meta gave its AI the green light to be 'sensual' with kids. Vice. Available from: vice.com/en/article/meta-gave-its-ai-the-green-light-to-be-sensual-with-kids/ [15 August 2025].

Preskill, J. (2018) Quantum computing in the NISQ era and beyond. *Quantum*, 2. 79. doi.org/10.22331/q-2018-08-06-79

Pudenz, K. L., Albash, T., and Lidar, D. A. (2014) Error-corrected quantum annealing with hundreds of qubits. *Nature*, 5. 3243. doi.org/10.1038/ncomms4243

Quantum Zeitgeist. (2024) Quantum computing and its ethical implications. Quantum Zeitgeist. Available from: quantumzeitgeist.com/quantum-computing-and-its-ethical-implications-2/ [18 August 2025].

Rabin, M. O. (1980) Probabilistic algorithm for testing primality. *Journal of Number Theory*, 12 (1). 128–138. doi.org/10.1016/0022-314X(80)90084-0

Raussendorf, R., and Briegel, H. J. (2001) A one-way quantum computer. *Physical Review Letters*, 86 (22). 5188. doi.org/10.1103/PhysRevLett.86.5188

Reddy, K. T., and Tschofenig, H. (2025) Post-quantum cryptography recommendations for TLS-based applications. Internet Engineering Task Force. ietf.org/archive/id/draft-ietf-uta-pqc-app-00.html

Rieffel, E., and Polak, W. (2011) *Quantum Computing: A Gentle Introduction*. Cambridge, MA: The MIT Press.

Robertson, A., Schaffner, C., and Verschoor, S. R. (2026) Integrity from algebraic manipulation detection in trusted-repeater QKD networks. Cryptographic ePrint archive. eprint.iacr.org/2026/092

Shor, P. W. (1994a) Polynomial time algorithms for discrete logarithms and factoring on a quantum computer. In *Proceedings of the First Algorithmic Number Theory Symposium*. 289–289.

Shor, P. W. (1994b) Algorithms for quantum computation: Discrete logarithms and factoring. In *Proceedings of the 26th ACM Symposium on the Theory of Computing*. ACM. 124–134.

Sikeridis, D., Kampanakis, P., and Devetsikiotis, M. (2020) Post-quantum authentication in TLS 1.3: A performance study. Network and Distributed Systems Security (NDSS) Symposium 2020.

Slussarenko, S., and Pryde, G. J. (2019) Photonic quantum information processing: A concise review. *Applied Physics Reviews*, 6 (4). 041303. doi.org/10.1063/1.5115814

Swayne, M. (2025) EU presses for quantum-safe encryption by 2030 as risks grow. *Quantum Insider*. Available from: thequantuminsider.com/2025/06/30/eu-presses-for-quantum-safe-encryption-by-2030-as-risks-grow/ [18 August 2025].

Venegas-Andraca, W., Cruz-Santos, S. E., McGeoch, C., and Lanzagorta, M. (2018) A cross-disciplinary introduction to quantum annealing-based algorithms. *Contemporary Physics*, 59 (2). 174–196. doi.org/10.1080/00107514.2018.1450720

Wintersperger, K., et al. (2023) Neutral atom quantum computing hardware: Performance and end-user perspective. *EPJ Quantum Technology*, 10. 32. doi.org/10.1140/epjqt/s40507-023-00190-1

Yanofsky, N. S., and Mannucci, M. A. (2012) *Quantum Computing for Computer Scientists*. Cambridge: Cambridge University Press. doi.org/10.1017/CBO9780511813887

Yin, J., et al. (2020) Entanglement-based secure quantum cryptography over 1,120 kilometres. *Nature*, 582. 501–505. doi.org/10.1038/s41586-020-2401-y

ABBREVIATIONS

AES	Advanced Encryption Standard
CLOPS	circuit layer operations per second
CPU	central processing unit
CRQC	cryptographically relevant quantum computer
CV	continuous variable
DLP	discrete logarithm problem
DNEL	deploy now, exploit later
DV	discrete variable
ECC	elliptic curve cryptography
ECDLP	elliptic curve discrete logarithm problem
ECDSA	elliptic curve digital signature algorithm
EPR	Einstein–Podolsky–Rosen
FIPS	Federal Information Processing Standard
FTQC	fault-tolerant quantum computing
GNFS	general number field sieve
GPU	graphics processing unit
HHL	Harrow–Hassidim–Lloyd
HNDL	harvest now, decrypt later
HNFL	harvest now, forge later
KLM	Knill–Laflamme–Milburn
LDPC	low-density parity-check
LOB	logical operations budget
LOQC	linear optical quantum computing

LQC	logical qubit capacity
MBQC	measurement-based quantum computing
ML-DSA	module-lattice-based digital signature algorithm
ML-KEM	module-lattice-based key encapsulation mechanism
NISQ	noisy intermediate-scale quantum
NIST	National Institute of Standards and Technology
PKI	public-key infrastructure
PQC	post-quantum cryptography
QAC	quantum annealing correction
QAOA	quantum approximate optimisation algorithm
QKD	quantum key distribution
QOT	quantum operations throughput
QUBO	quadratic unconstrained Boolean optimisation
RSA	Rivest–Shamir–Adleman
SAT	satisfiability
SHA	secure hash algorithm
SLH-DSA	stateless hash-based digital signature algorithm
TI	trapped ion
TLS	Transport Layer Security
TNFL	trust now, forge later
VUCA	volatile, uncertain, complex and ambiguous

GLOSSARY

Adiabatic computing: A quantum computing method where we start the Hamiltonian in a known state and evolve it slowly (thus avoiding quantum jumps) into the Hamiltonian for the desired state.

Advanced Encryption Standard (AES): The most commonly used block cipher. Somewhat vulnerable to Grover's algorithm (see Chapter 4).

Annealing: A heat treatment that alters the material properties of a material. Simulated annealing is an optimisation algorithm loosely inspired by this, and quantum annealing is a quantum equivalent.

APX-hard: Those problems that are asymptotically at least as hard as all problems that have polynomial-time bounded-relative error approximation algorithms. See Definition 3.9, p. 93 of Ausiello et al. (1999).

Bit: A value that is either definitely 0 or definitely 1. Contrast with qubit.

Bloch sphere: A representation of a quantum state as a point on the surface of a sphere (see Chapter 1).

Crypto agility: The ability to change cryptographic keys/algorithms easily.

Decoherence: The loss of information from qubits to the environment.

Deploy now, exploit later (DNEL): The situation where we are deploying vulnerable cryptography now, especially in physical devices that will be hard to upgrade (see Chapter 6).

Dirac notation: A notation for vectors etc., commonly used in quantum mechanics (see Chapter 4).

DiVincenzo criteria: Seven conditions required in order to successfully implement a quantum algorithm. See DiVincenzo (1997).

Elliptic curve cryptography (ECC): The basis of current public-key cryptography, but easily broken by Shor's algorithm.

Entanglement: The quantum state of each particle in an entangled group cannot be described independently of the states of the other members of the group (see Chapter 1).

Error correction: The ability of a system to correct some errors in its computation or data communication.

Factorisation: Decomposing an integer into the primes that multiply together to give that integer.

GPU: Originally just a graphics processing unit; now, a specific kind of processor often used for machine learning applications.

Ground state: The state of lowest energy of a quantum system. To be contrasted with 'excited state'.

Grover's algorithm: A quantum algorithm for finding inputs to functions that give certain answers (see Chapter 4).

Hadamard gate: A quantum gate that transforms the states $|0\rangle$ and $|1\rangle$ to $|+\rangle$ and $|-\rangle$, called h and h' in Chapter 4, p. 32.

Hamiltonian: An operator representing the total energy of a system (see Chapter 4).

Harrow–Hassidim–Lloyd (HHL) algorithm: Can find eigenvalues of a matrix exponentially faster than classical algorithms (see Chapter 3).

Harvest now, decrypt later (HNDL): Collect encrypted data of long-term value and decrypt it when a suitable quantum computer becomes available (see Chapter 6).

Harvest now, forge later (HNFL): Collect cryptographically signed data of long-term value and forge equivalently valuable data when a suitable quantum computer becomes available (see Chapter 6).

Holevo bound: An upper bound on the amount of classical information that can be transmitted by quantum means. If A and B are communicating using n qubits, though these can carry much more information, the amount of classical information that can be retried by B from one transmission by A is bounded by 2^n, i.e. the same as n classical bits.

Josephson junction: A nonlinear, dissipationless circuit element consisting of a weak barrier (such as an insulator) separating two superconductors. It is a key element of a superconducting qubit.

Linear optical quantum computing (LOQC): A key technology for photonic qubits (see Chapter 5).

Logical qubit: A construction that behaves like an error-free qubit. Compare 'physical qubit'.

Measurement: Looking at a qubit, or set of qubits, which forces them into a definitive state. 'When we open the box, Schrödinger's cat is either definitely alive or definitely dead.'

Measurement-based quantum computing (MBQC): A formulation often used in LOQC, where the basic operation is formed by entangling the input qubits with ancilla qubits, doing some measurements, and then regarding the other qubits as output (see Chapter 5).

Noise: The external conditions that might cause a physical qubit to behave differently from the ideal state.

Noisy intermediate-scale quantum (NISQ): Computer, the sort that are actually available in 2026.

NP: The class of problems that can be solved in polynomial time on a non-deterministic Turing machine; equivalently those whose solution can be verified in polynomial time on a deterministic Turing machine.

NP-hard: A problem that is, asymptotically, at least as hard as all NP problems. An NP-hard problem may not be in NP. A problem that is in NP and is NP-hard is known as NP-complete.

Photonics: The use of photons (light particles), in particular to carry qubits.

Physical qubit: A physical construct that carries a quantum bit but is subject to errors.

Post-quantum cryptography (PQC): The cryptography we can do now, on classical computers, that is sufficiently safe against an opponent with a quantum computer (see Chapter 6).

Quantum advantage: When a quantum computer can perform a task faster than a classical computer. Not a very well-defined concept.

Quantum annealer: Quantum optimisation technique based on classical computing's 'simulated annealing'. See Annealing.

Quantum approximate optimisation algorithm (QAOA): An alternative to quantum annealing that runs on standard gate-model quantum hardware (see p. 31).

Quantum gate: The basic element of a quantum circuit.

Quantum key distribution: A quantum mechanism whereby two parties can establish a shared key while being sufficiently certain that this has not been intercepted (see Chapter 4).

Quantum mechanics: The physics of quantum events.

Quantum oracle: A quantum circuit for a function *f* that takes a (superposition) input *x* and returns the corresponding superposition *f*(*x*).

Quantum supremacy: More than quantum advantage; when a quantum computer can solve problems that a classical computer cannot solve in 'reasonable time'.

Qubit: A 'quantum bit', which has some probability of being measured as 0 and a corresponding probability of being measured as 1.

Qubit connectivity: In an actual quantum machine, the connectivity tells us which qubits can connect directly with which others.

Rivest–Shamir–Adleman (RSA): The original public-key signature scheme, now largely replaced by ECC. Vulnerable to Shor's algorithm.

Satisfiability: Can a Boolean expression be made true (satisfied) by a choice of values true/false for the variables?

Schrödinger's cat: An analogy for superposition, where the cat is both alive and dead until we open the box it is in.

Shor's algorithm: A family of algorithms that can break RSA and ECC (see Chapter 4).

Superposition: The situation where a set of classical bits has several possibilities, but the corresponding set of qubits has all these possibilities, each with a certain probability (often equal probability).

Transpilation: The process of rewriting a given input quantum circuit to match the topology (quantum connectivity) of a specific quantum device (see Chapter 5).

Trapped-ion qubits: One possible hardware implementation of quantum computing (see Chapter 5).

Trust now, forge later (TNFL): The situation where we trust digital signatures, etc. now, but a sufficiently powerful quantum computer will be able to forge them in the future (see Chapter 6).

Published by BCS Learning and Development Ltd, a wholly owned subsidiary of BCS, The Chartered Institute for IT, 3 Newbridge Square, Swindon, SN1 1BY, UK.
bcs.org

EU GPSR Authorised Representative: LOGOS EUROPE, 9 Rue Nicolas Poussin, 17000 La Rochelle, France.
Contact@logoseurope.eu

Paperback ISBN: 978-1-78017-6765
PDF ISBN: 978-1-78017-6772
ePUB ISBN: 978-1-78017-6789

Ebook available

British Cataloguing in Publication Data.
A CIP catalogue record for this book is available at the British Library.

Publisher's acknowledgements
Reviewers: Katie Walsh, Kate Baucherel, Nick Colosimo
Publisher: Ian Borthwick
Commissioning editor: Heather Wood
Production manager: Florence Leroy
Project manager: Sunrise Setting Ltd
Copy-editor: Richard Hutchinson
Proofreader: Graham Frankland
Cover design: Alex Wright
Cover image: iStock/StationaryTraveller
Typeset by Lapiz Digital Services, Chennai, India

BCS, THE CHARTERED INSTITUTE FOR IT

BCS, The Chartered Institute for IT, is committed to making IT good for society. We use the power of our network to bring about positive, tangible change. We champion the global IT profession and the interests of individuals, engaged in that profession, for the benefit of all.

Exchanging IT expertise and knowledge

The Institute fosters links between experts from industry, academia and business to promote new thinking, education and knowledge sharing.

Supporting practitioners

Through continuing professional development and a series of respected IT qualifications, the Institute seeks to promote professional practice tuned to the demands of business. It provides practical support and information services to its members and volunteer communities around the world.

Setting standards and frameworks

The Institute collaborates with government, industry and relevant bodies to establish good working practices, codes of conduct, skills frameworks and common standards. It also offers a range of consultancy services to employers to help them adopt best practice.

Become a member

Over 70,000 people including students, teachers, professionals and practitioners enjoy the benefits of BCS membership. These include access to an international community, invitations to a roster of local and national events, career development tools and a quarterly thought-leadership magazine. Visit bcs.org to find out more.

Further information

BCS, The Chartered Institute for IT,
3 Newbridge Square,
Swindon, SN1 1BY, United Kingdom.
T +44 (0) 1793 417 417
(Monday to Friday, 09:00 to 17:00 UK time)
bcs.org/contact

shop.bcs.org/
publishing@bcs.uk

bcs.org/qualifications-and-certifications/certifications-for-professionals/

www.ingramcontent.com/pod-product-compliance
Lightning Source LLC
LaVergne TN
LVHW052338100826
845147LV00020B/1102